There You Have It
A Real Raw Candid Look Into My Crazy Life

Copyright © 2025 by Kristi Lyons

All rights reserved.

No part of this publication may be reproduced, distributed, or transmitted in any form or by any means, including photocopying, recording, or other electronic or mechanical methods, without the prior written permission of the author, except in the case of brief quotations used in reviews, articles, or scholarly works.

Disclaimer

This book is a collection of Danielle's personal experiences and life lessons. She's not an expert—just someone who's been through a lot and wants to share what she's learned along the way. The stories and insights are meant to encourage, inspire, and spark reflection, but they're not a substitute for professional advice, diagnosis, or treatment.

Contents

	VI
Preface	1
Introduction	3
1. Who is Danielle Behar Salinger?	7
2. The Sole Sister	11
3. Growing Up an Eighties Girl	16
4. The School Playground Echo: A Letter to My Younger Me	21
5. The Space She Left Behind: An Unspoken Goodbye	26
6. More Than Mother and Child: The Friendship That Unfolded	31
7. Beneath the Surface: The Hidden Life of My Dad	36
8. Embracing Loss - My Journey	41
9. Blended Not Brewed: The Awkward Salinger Potluck	46
10. Shining a Light on My Legacy: The Jewish Roots	51
11. Dan & Danielle: A Love Story with Extra Steps and a Salinger Twist	57
12. Our Wedding Day	63
13. First Love, Then Kids	68
14. The Story Deepens and Endures	77
15. Pieces of Ed: Through the Fog: Navigating Dementia with Ed	83

16.	The Ed-ventures of Caregiving: Ed-ucating Ourselves Through Colliding Hardships, Hilarity, and Heartfelt Moments	88
17.	Women With Defining Influence	94
18.	The Power of Every Step: Danielle, Leading With Every Treadmill Stride	99
19.	A Snapshot Of A Day In The Life of 'Me'	105
20.	Shifting Gears: Trading the Corporate 9-to-5 for Full-Time Mom-a-Care-Duty-Influencer	111
21.	Zoomies	116
22.	Hot Flashes & Hot Takes: Menopause Madness You're Valid, You're Worthy, and Yes, You're Still Fabulous (Even When Sweating!)	122
23.	A New Reality: Navigating the Unseen Pain of Fibromyalgia Discovering Fibromyalgia	129
24.	From Steps on the Treadmill to Cash Talk & Bank Accounts	134
25.	Hair Today, Strands Gone Tomorrow: The Letting-Go Journey	141
26.	Embracing Aging and Real Beauty	147
27.	Friendship: Through Thick and Thin, Laughter and Pain, Honey and Vinegar, Memories and Milestones	152
28.	Hold That Thought... I Want To, But I'm Not Listening Anyway	159
29.	Not Wrong, Just Different	164
30.	Unity Despite Politics	170
31.	No Two Happy Places Are Alike	176
32.	Forgiveness & Releasing The Hearts Burden	181
33.	Trolls, Bullies, and What is a Ninny? Oh My! How We Handle It All with Humor Armor	187
34.	Fit, Fierce, and Balanced: The Fitness & Wellness Duo	193

35.	Kindness In Action: A Daily Choice	199
36.	Randomness	203
	About the authors	208
	About the authors (Part 2)	210
	Acknowledgements	212
	Closing Thoughts	213
	What's next?	
	Thank You!	214
	A Personal Note From Danielle	

Life doesn't follow our plans.
Sometimes it drags us through chaos,
other times it surprises us with joy.
Either way, we keep going. This is my story.
— Danielle

Preface

I still remember the first time I saw Danielle Salinger on YouTube. I was immediately drawn in by her sincerity, especially how she handled a tender moment with her father-in-law, Ed. At that time, she was just beginning her digital journey, and we had only seen a glimpse of what was to come. As I continued to follow the Salingers, I found something genuinely authentic in what she and her husband Dan bring to the world of social media. The way Ed shuffled around reminded me so much of my grandfather after he was diagnosed with Alzheimer's. He even bore a slight resemblance to my uncle. Those familiar connections, the gestures, the expressions, the quiet dignity—kept me watching.

As much as I loved the combined Salinger videos, I was stoked when Danielle started working out with us daily on her own channel! She brought the perfect mix of motivation and fun, creating an atmosphere that made tuning in feel exciting. What inspired me even more was how courageously she has lived so many roles—wife, mother, daughter, granddaughter, sister, aunt, employee, caretaker, homemaker, and more. There was so much in her conversations that I could relate to.

So why would anyone care about her story? Danielle is a well-rounded woman with a lot inside of her to give. I've found that I have so much in common with her, and the more I hear about her life, the more I want to know. No matter who you are, there is sure to be something you will relate to in this book.

When I think of Danielle, I think of a real, straightforward woman who is an overcomer of much! You don't have to wonder if she's being honest; that's what makes her a gem in a world of counterfeits. She is legit. I admire Danielle for tackling the obstacles with great resilience despite the hindrances along the way.

Today, she lives in the limelight of many phones, tablets, computers, and television sets. At times, it seems like some people go out of their way to dim her light with constant trolling. There isn't much escape in the digital world. But still, strolling along despite it all is a woman with dignity—a lady who would rather face a little bit of sourness while making efforts to bring some sweetness into this world. Any turmoil she may endure isn't worth giving up the impact she has already made, and she continues in her pursuit to stay genuine while knocking down a few monsters along the way.

You picked up a great read by choosing Danielle's story! This book is about staying on your path, no matter what you run into along the way—and doing it in a way that's true to who you are. It's amazing that I ended up following her journey, and not only did we connect, but I would later be writing a book with her. Who knew? We found so many similarities, even down to being born in the same year. Two very different people, yet with so much in common. We literally live across the country from one another (NY to California). It was almost an instant bond and understanding between us—truly destined.

Beyond the final chapter, we can only anticipate even more inspiration coming from the livestreams ahead and the incredible content being created. The story doesn't end here—it's just the beginning!

Kristi Lyons

Introduction

In a universe that can sometimes feel like it's throwing pies of doubt in your face, some stories shine as bright as a lighthouse on a shore. When the forces of the trolls from Earth have teamed up to "tag you it" for their chaos, there are still stories that remind you to duck, dodge, and keep going.

This is one of those stories. My name is Danielle Salinger. A wife, mother, daughter-in-law, sister-in-law, sister, aunt, stepsister, caretaker, social media lady, grocery gatherer, and I have many more hats with titles on them hanging above my treadmill in my garage. I'm being silly with that one! You get my point. I joined the Fifty Club not too long ago and you can find me at my homestead in Elk Grove, California.

What you hold in your hands is a compilation of experiences and lessons learned and a testimony to the unstoppable force of persistence. It's a story that gets it—those calm, cool, collected moments that flip into chaos in a flash. The everything-all-at-once kind of stuff. Like when you're already running late and suddenly can't find your keys, all while slowly ticking through a mental checklist that somehow makes them even harder to find. And then, out of nowhere, it hits you—did I leave the oven on? Or... was it just the oven light. It's not really about dramatic twists or perfect endings. It's about the real-life moments that sneak up on us—shaping our days, our months, our whole lives. The moments we carry quietly until they need to become something bigger. Stories we have to share—so we know we're not the only ones feeling a little crazy, and neither is anyone else.

Life, as I've understood it, is like a paintball game you didn't even know you were playing. One where you're constantly dodging unexpected shots and figuring out which direction to run next. From those moments when you're on top of the world to the next that hit you where you weren't covered and wonder how you'll get up. My journey has been anything but linear. Each splatter of paint that has come my way has helped color the canvas of what I'm sharing. Now, we won't go and relive every brutal hit, but we'll look at how I had to duck, reload, and keep moving forward. Even when my armor was slightly dented, I used it as an experience to learn how to adjust my shield, my attitude, or my approach and patch it up. The dents may be invisible scars, but the resilience forged through them remains unmistakable.

As you turn through the pages of my book, you'll discover some of the hardcore stories of struggle and success, dreams that were deferred and realized, and failures that became the foundation for future victories. Through these chapters, I hope you'll find a reflection of your own journey and the courage to press on, no matter how steep the climb may seem. I invite you to join me as I revisit the highs and lows of my life, hoping that my experiences can serve as inspiration and empowerment.

We are here now despite how you may have found your way to my book – and I'm glad you are. It could be the right words of the algorithm in your search that recommended it, you have been waiting to read it, or you love a good read that doesn't end with something unrealistic. I've certainly faced my share of challenges, and with each chapter, I hope you find a space that invites you to dig a little deeper into yourself, encouraging reflection and deeper introspection. Who knows, this might even bring you to a turning point that makes you rethink everything you thought you knew about me—in the best way possible! (But hey, if you thought I was a total hot mess, maybe with this raw, candid look, you'll start to see the charm...) It's not just a book, but it embraces my learning experiences—written to challenge assumptions, share my truth, awaken new perspectives, and spark something inside of you.

Now, get ready—prepare yourself... and your mind (yep, I said it, your mind)! The chairlift is rising, and this journey is about to take off! Buckle up, because this is a ride that might just stick with you long after you turn the last page—something you'll want to reread, reshare, and hey, maybe even buy a copy for your friend!

1
Who is Danielle Behar Salinger?

A fun Danielle fact: I didn't have a nickname when I was young, and we won't dive into the details of how it came to be, but in high school and still today, some friends affectionately call me "Beanie." It's just a playful reminder of my younger years.
Danielle

My name is Danielle Rachel Behar Salinger. I was born to my parents, Janice and Pierre, on May 5th, 1974, at Baptist Hospital in Tennessee. My mother didn't often talk about my delivery. Still, she did share a funny memory: when I was born, she looked at me and said, "Is this my monkey?" because I was quite hairy!

Today, I live in Elk Grove, California, with my family. It's a place where life is fast paced, and no two days are exactly the same. You'll learn more about me and my family in the chapters to come—quirks, stories, and unforgettable moments that have made life special. There's so much to share, and I'm excited to bring you along for the ride!

My mother, Janice Seidner Behar Salinger, was born in Italy to Jack and Sara Seidner. She was an amazing woman—the calmest and most collected person I've ever known—passive and mellow yet full of an upbeat spirit. Her reassuring mantra was always, "Don't worry; it will all work out." She had an incredible ability to make everything seem manageable, no matter how difficult things got.

My father, Pierre Alan Behar, was a very handsome man, born in Cairo, Egypt, to my grandparents, Lola and Albert Behar, during a time of war. He was the baby of three children, his older siblings being Ray and Nicole. When that conflict finally subsided, his family, once wealthy, had lost everything as a result of the war. They made their way across the globe to the United States, starting in New York, New Jersey, and eventually settling in Tennessee.

Dad had so much charisma and charm and a way of captivating everyone who encountered him. His infectious energy drew people in; anyone who had the pleasure of knowing him could be mesmerized with his instant charm. He had a way of lighting up a room, making conversations feel effortless with how engaging he was. With a warm smile and an adventurous spirit, his presence was magnetic. My dad's ability to connect left a lasting impression on all who crossed his path.

I've always looked up to my mom's mother—my maternal grandmother, Sara—because she was an extraordinary woman, full of resilience and grace. Born in Italy, she and my grandfather were shaped by the hardships they faced during the war. It was a true test of strength and determination. Together, they built a loving family, welcoming five children—Janice, Betty, Helen, Leo, and Sam—into the world. After the war, they made the courageous journey to Ellis Island, seeking a fresh start. And what better place to begin again than America—a land long seen as full of promise and possibility? Eventually, they settled in Tennessee, where their story of perseverance and love took root. That story continues to inspire our family to this day.

So, my mother and father's paths eventually crossed in Nashville—a city that became the backdrop for their love story. It feels almost poetic to think about how two individuals from different continents and very different backgrounds found their way to each other, and how an unexpected spark of attraction brought them together. I often think about how incredible it is that if even one of them had stayed behind—in Italy or Cairo—their journeys never would have led to the vibrant heart of Nashville, where their lives would eventually intertwine in ways only fate could orchestrate. And if their lives had never merged, there would be no Danielle Salinger! Their connection not only made my existence possible, but it also reminds me to stay open—and to never underestimate the power of the unexpected. Life has a way of weaving stories and histories together in the most neat and wondrous ways. Their migration shows how life's beautiful coincidences can unite entirely different worlds, resulting in something truly magical.

I was the only child that my mother and father had together. When I was born, my parents had not yet decided on a name for me, so I arrived at the hospital without one. Fortunately, my dad's sister (my Aunt Nicole), who was familiar with our family naming traditions, stepped in to choose a name. Danielle was original; my middle name, Rachel, was after my great-grandmother.

As the first grandchild on my mother's side, I was showered with attention and affection. I also had two aunts who were not much older than me, creating a unique bond and camaraderie. One thing that turned out great for my mom was that she had plenty of help in caring for me, thanks to this close-knit family.

When I reflect back on my mom and dad's marriage, I know there was something between them, but it was not long-lasting. When my mother met my father, she had recently ended her relationship with the one who was her first love. Mom was faced with the decision to wait for him to finish medical school or to move on. She chose the latter. My dad became her rebound. She was eager to love, but in the end, she was not willing to wait for what her heart desired the most. The marriage between my parents lasted only about 18 months.

When my mother saw my dad, she noticed that he was quite handsome. Add to that his irresistible charm, and it was pure allure. But no amount of anything from my father could replace what she once had with her first love, and I believe that was a significant part of why things didn't last for very long between my parents.

They were two young people who were clinging to the idea of an ideal love, but they experienced anything but the real thing. The relationship was built upon what might have been instead of what truly was. My mother probably envisioned her fairy tale love to have been a completely different scenario and regretted some of her decisions. However, the path of their short-lived love led to my existence, and I am truly grateful for that.

If you were to ask me now whether I was saddened by my parents' divorce, I didn't have the experience of knowing what it was like for them to be married, as I was too young to remember much. I was surrounded by so much love that the divorce didn't significantly impact me. I didn't know anything different, so how could I really talk about it? While my life was affected by divorce, I didn't experience it in a way that left me feeling hurt. My dad was present in my life, and I knew I had him.

Do you ever find it hard to express how you may have felt about parts of your childhood when someone asks? I think it can be tough to pinpoint those emotions being so long ago. The mind can get a little fuzzy. When people ask about your early years, do you ever struggle to answer, or do certain questions make you pause? I find this particularly when it comes to family stuff or remembering big moments. While photos or videos can help, there are finer details that fade with time.

Even when we can't recall everything fully, the earliest experiences of our lives can shape us. We may be able to tap into some deeper emotions when we encounter thought provoking questions about our childhood or hear stories. Sometimes memories bring to mind the complexities that came with our upbringing. It's important to acknowledge that any feelings around it still matter, even if they aren't tied to any specific event. These reflections can influence the understanding we have of who we are today.

Some people may want everyone to think they had the perfect upbringing, but I believe we all carry our own baggage. Many might romanticize the idea of having the ideal mother and father. Still, the reality is that no one has it all figured out. Life is filled with difficulties and imperfections. Acknowledging this helps us embrace our own experiences, however flawed they may be. We can remind ourselves that growth often comes from embracing the facts of what we do know—and being okay with what we may never fully understand.

"Throughout this journey, my perspective has shifted. Even though my identity has been tested, stretched, broken, and ultimately healed; in the end I've become more authentically me— more Danielle than I've ever been before." Danielle

2
The Sole Sister

The bloodline is everything—your roots, your identity, and the core of who you are. It's often the strongest, most meaningful connection you have to the past. Though we aren't always closest to those by blood, that bond still holds deep significance. Danielle

Being that I was the only girl among all younger brothers—and with a big age gap—gave me a unique childhood. Some people say having a sister would've changed everything, but would it have? Hard to say. I've heard sisters can have a special bond, but the connection with my brothers turned out to be quite meaningful.

I've always tried to see the bright side. Without a sister, I avoided jealousy, competition, or drama. No one snuck stuff out of my closet—though having an older sister to borrow things from might've been cool. That just wasn't my reality, and honestly, I was fine with it.

Those early years felt quiet, even dull at times. There were no shared sleeping bags on camping trips or mall drop-offs with a sister. No sibling pranks, I didn't have to share a room or deal with that classic rivalry. On road trips, it was just me in the back seat—probably a blessing in disguise since I had no one to tease me or tattletale. Not having a built-in playmate or someone to pass clothes down to came with its own mix of feelings, but it all shaped my world for the first ten years of life.

Where I could, I compensated with friendships. The kids I spent time with helped fill the gaps left by the absence of siblings my own age. I wasn't the kid with a treehouse or a big backyard full of adventure. Instead, I played in bushes, parking lots—wherever we could make fun happen. A lot of those memories are vague, and truthfully, I prefer not to dwell on them too much. But I do remember the comforting scent of my mom's Fendi perfume lingering through the house as I bounced in and out, and the simple joy of riding my bike. Hopscotch and roller skating were favorites, and I especially loved it when my mom and I went rollerblading together.

Ah, to think back to those days! We'd rush to grab the garden hose for a cold drink on a hot day, never questioning if it was safe. It was always a race to get home before the streetlights flickered on—that was the rule! Such iconic memories of childhood freedom and simpler times. There was some kind of magic in those summer evenings. Life was rather straightforward, and adventure felt endless. Growing up in the seventies and eighties, being outside was truly the heart of childhood. We played hopscotch, hide-and-seek, enjoyed skateboarding, riding bikes, or bouncing a ball in the community basketball hoop. It would've felt odd to stay inside because the outdoors offered so much freedom and creativity.

Baking never really interested me, but I spent a lot of time by my mom's side in the kitchen, just watching her cook. One of her most cherished dishes—stuffed cabbage—was passed down from my grandmother and is still a family favorite. I also have sweet memories of doing word searches and puzzles with my grandfather. And from early on, Yahtzee was—and still is—my favorite game.

Josh came along when I was 10, and having a little brother was pretty neat. Big sister duties felt fun, and being in the same house let us create a special connection—just the two of us, in our own way, as big sister and little brother.

I also have two other younger brothers, Michael and Matthew, from my dad and Barbara (aka Babs). They grew up living in Tennessee and were relatively younger than me as well. I only saw them during summer trips. Because of the age gap between us, it's pretty hard to remember much beyond the time spent playing outside during my visits. It wasn't until we grew older that we began to bridge those gaps, realizing our connections deepened as we shared more relatable life experiences.

It was time for me to move out when I came to a certain age. Josh was still young, but I made a point to stay involved in his life. As he grew up, there are fond memories of attending some of his sporting events like wrestling and baseball, and I always felt the need to keep an eye on him. Even though I didn't live in the house anymore, there was still a strong bond. I'll always cherish the moments I spent with him, even the typical little brother antics that came with the territory. The relationship I share with Josh to this day has always been especially close.

My connection with Matthew and Mikey is rooted in love. After our father passed away in 2008, it truly changed the dynamic of our relationship. What had once been the familiar routine of annual summer visits transformed into facing one of the hardest moments of our lives. His death caused something deeply profound to shift within us.

His loss created a void that brought us closer in ways we had never experienced. We were faced with overwhelming emotions, especially since Dad was so young and we, particularly my younger brothers, were incredibly young to be losing him. For the first time, we had to process such intense feelings together as siblings. Sharing this loss forced us to rely on one another for support, and as we confronted the reality of our new circumstances, deeper connections began to form.

Then came a moment that brought us together in a way never expected. Dad had always wanted to take us to Mexico, but he didn't get a chance to before he passed away. So, Barbara (Babs), being clever, came up with an idea. We went to Lake Tahoe, where Matthew and Michael rented a boat for the occasion. What followed became an unforgettable experience—marked by humor and chaos. It was one of the most significant moments of our lives: the attempt to release Dad's ashes. He had always expressed a wish for his ashes to be scattered in a meaningful place, and we were determined to honor that wish and the deep connection he wanted to maintain with us.

With no anticipation of how difficult it would be trying to do so on a windy day, such a simple task of releasing ashes turned into a repetitive struggle. We battled gusts that sent the ashes swirling unpredictably everywhere you can imagine, even into our mouths. It was such a scene mixed with anguish, humor, and comedy. Despite encountering less-than-ideal conditions that day, it became a beloved memory that will be carried with us for all our lives. That moment still brings laughter to this day. This is one more reminder of life's unpredictability and how we can find humor even amid the most troubling situations. Having that experience with my brothers and stepmom gave us the love, laughter, and closeness our dad would have wanted us to have for years to come.

So, there you have it: growing up as the only sister was quite alright, shaped by the many moments and interactions I had. But once my siblings came into my life, I wasn't quite so "sole" anymore. There are so many stories to tell. While I technically wasn't an only child—since I had younger brothers—I can definitely relate to how being the oldest, the youngest, or even an only child can stir up feelings of independence or isolation. Each of us experiences life through our own lens, and those perspectives are what make our journeys so interesting.

We don't get to choose our birth order, how many brothers or sisters we have, or the situational aspects of our family. It's always fascinating to hear the stories of others. For someone in a large family, it might have felt confined or overwhelming, especially if they wished for one or two siblings instead of ten. On the flip side, an only child might have longed for siblings but also reveled in the perks of having all the attention and being spoiled.

How do you think that significant age differences can affect relationships with siblings? We might not have been close-knit from the get-go, and there are a lot of complexities. Still, over time, with a desire for a deeper connection, this type of sibling experience isn't so bad. I see that, especially now. Of course, I dealt with it both near and far – with one brother living with me in California and the others in Tennessee.

Like me, can you relate to being a "sole sister?" Maybe being the only child, or it felt that way because your siblings were much older or much younger. That can create a type of "only child isolation" that affects your life in various ways. Did you see any pros and cons to it? No, I wasn't an only child, but I've heard there is a certain stigma attached with being one.

Our world paints an idea of what family and siblings are supposed to look like, but reality doesn't always match that picture. If you didn't have siblings, it's okay. The connections you create aren't limited by that. Whether with family, friends, or others who become like family, the bonds you build are just as meaningful and deeply impactful. It's never too late to create the kind of relationships you long for—those that feel genuine and fulfilling. Your worth and your place in this world are defined not by your family structure, but by who you are, the love you share, and the quiet strength you carry within.

3
Growing Up an Eighties Girl

The world is your oyster. The world is in your hands. It's all in how you make an effort and what you put into it. Be independent. Love with depth and abandon, because tomorrow is never promised. But also build a life that stands strong, even if you're ever standing alone. That is what my mother taught me and I'm sticking with it. Danielle

Growing up as a teenager in the eighties was an amazing experience in what is known today as the retro time period. It was a decade so rad, those who didn't live it will never be able to understand what made it unforgettable. This was the time before the digital age took over. We were raised with old-fashioned values and watched family television shows like *Full House* and *The Cosby Show*, which were central to our lives. I miss that simplicity and wish my kids could have experienced it for themselves. We would often watch TV in the evenings with our family members. The television shows back then had a strong emphasis on family values and the relationships that were created inside the family unit. In the brief span of a half-hour episode, a challenge would arise and be resolved. The family dynamic was always something relatable in its own tacky way. The themes were more based on love, personal growth, and conflict resolution within your relationships. These shows offered something that was structured on the importance of family. You could easily relate to something you would see on the screen and reflect from what you learned in the story. It would provide a sense of fullness that left you feeling optimistic and uplifted.

I remember magazines like *Bop, Teen Beat,* and *Seventeen*. They were loaded with all kinds of fun content and most likely you could find something on every page to your liking. We would read articles of the interviews with our favorite pop stars and actors. There were posters and pictures for us to tear out and hang up to decorate our bedrooms at home or lockers at school. In the back of most any magazine, they provided us addresses where we could send fan letters to our favorite stars. We had the opportunity to join fan clubs for a small fee and get monthly newsletters with a picture or a small special gift inside the envelope in association with that particular club. It was always something that we could look forward to each month. The magazines also gave us cool fashion tips, along with games and quizzes to help us learn more about our favorite celebrities. It was innocent and fun!

Beyond the television set there were so many fun aspects to life in the eighties. I found that there was something special about riding in the back of a pickup truck or writing in cursive—simple joys that seem to be lost with today's generation. Back then, life was straightforward and low maintenance. We had meaningful conversations and valued real connections over material possessions. Today, it feels like life is more complicated; people are constantly juggling finances, comparing themselves to others, and always wanting more. I think regardless of our family's income, we all felt we had more than we actually did.

If you lived through school in the eighties, you knew what the "Pizza Hut Book It" program was. We had the incentive to read because most all schools were partnered with their local Pizza Hut. Teachers would sign up their classes and then hand out large round pins, where students could proudly place their star stickers that tracked accomplishments. After reading a set number of books, we would gain our achievement certificate and be able to redeem it for a free personal pan pizza. Having that memory instantly links us back to a positive literacy connection, in that reading brought forth to us delicious rewards!

Mail order record clubs offered a thrill while eagerly waiting for cassettes or compact discs to arrive in the mail. While solving the Rubik's cube was popular for some, my personal memories revolve around mall trips, movies, and hanging out. I loved all kinds of eighties music, especially pop, and enjoyed the era's pop culture: from *Three's Company* and *Family Ties* to Cabbage Patch Dolls, Barbie, Garbage Pail Kids, Strawberry Shortcake, and Smurfs. Saturday mornings were filled with excitement for a few hours, then it was off to making or swapping bracelets and having fun. Nowadays, it feels like we've traded those puddles of joy for pools of complexity and discontent.

Most girls in the eighties had a sticker book. It's a cherished pastime of mine, for sure. If you weren't a girl in that era with a sticker book in hand, you missed one of the sparkly parts of growing up. Stickers back then were fairly inexpensive, making them accessible to just about everyone, regardless of household income. We had the coolest stickers to trade, collect, and showcase in our albums. Hours were spent arranging our sticker books in ways that expressed each of our personalities. We'd make special trips to the mall to visit the specialty shop that offered a wide variety of stickers, all tied to the popular culture of the time. We'd roam the store, carefully browsing and selecting our treasures to add to our collections when we got home. There were scratch-and-sniff stickers, poofy ones, rainbow designs in all kinds of shapes, and even some with ink inside that shifted when pressed. Animal stickers, cartoon characters, TV stars – oh yes, there was something for everyone. The best way I can describe it is like walking into a craft store filled with endless reels of fabric—only for us, it was reels of stickers galore. Honestly, every one of them seemed like a must have.

From boom boxes and jelly shoes to emulating Molly Ringwald's style and dreaming of romances like those in *The Karate Kid*, the eighties were a time of bold fashion and cinematic aspirations. The stories that were on the big screen were created to resonate deeply inside of us, capturing both our struggles along with the dreams we held.

We were excited to head to the video store when the movie came out on VHS tape. We couldn't wait to watch *Dirty Dancing* or *Ferris Bueller's Day Off* and repeat those fun movies shown at the theatre a few months before.

Most video stores had freshly made popcorn that they gave out for free when we rented two videos or more. It allowed us to have that movie experience in its own distinct way. When someone rented a video, everyone at home typically watched it together or sometimes invited friends over to join. Getting in as many viewings as possible seemed to be the goal before returning the movies.

We had iconic toys, MTV revolutionized music videos, and TV dinners were a staple of our meals. Face-to-face interactions were the norm, a concept so different from today's digital world. The idea of a mobile phone seemed almost futuristic, with the exception of my friend's dad who had one of those impressive car phones that came in a large bag. Socializing in high school meant actually dating or talking to people in person. We wrote notes and passed them in the halls, creating connections in a way that feels almost quaint now. And yes, I lived through that era—big hair and all. I definitely rocked the voluminous look with netted hairspray, embracing every quintessential detail of eighties style.

Creating our own mixtapes in the eighties was an activity that most of us loved to do. We would eagerly wait for a specific favorite to come on the radio, and then press the record button to capture the song on the blank cassette. Each mixtape was like a custom soundtrack, a variety of songs that represented our tastes and complemented our memories. Artists like Madonna, Michael Jackson, Howard Jones, and the Pet Shop Boys dominated the airwaves, and their songs often found a place on our mixes. Some tapes we made just for ourselves, but others were created with someone special in mind, a crush, a best friend, or someone we simply didn't have the words to say out loud to. Instead, we'd let the lyrics do the talking for us. Our tapes were often a blend of upbeat hits and sentimental slow songs, capturing everything we were feeling at the time. Listening to one now would be like opening a time capsule—a vivid snapshot of a youthful moment of expression. And for the especially creative among us, blending tracks together became an art of its own.

Teens of the eighties would spend a lot of time hanging out at the mall, and drive-in theaters were a popular spot. We'd spend hours in the arcades, watching each other play while leaning on the side of the machine with our heads tilted over. While at the mall we would explore our favorite clothing stores. Back then the fashion styles consisted of big sweatshirts, stonewashed jeans, stirrup pants, and other trends that were often influenced by celebrities like Madonna. Earrings and necklaces in the eighties were big, bold, and colorful. The more layers you wore, the better. This plentiful, vibrant style perfectly reflected the bold fashion trends of that time.

Brands like Guess and Esprit were big back in the eighties. Perms were very popular as well. It wasn't rare to see crimped or zigzag hair, side ponytails that were kept in place with big scrunchies, or hair feathered in the middle. When it came to makeup, the brighter, the better. There were a lot of pastel shades in the stores, and it was pretty normal to apply our blush fairly heavy.

I feel like the bonds among friends were formed because of our interests in similar things. It could have been fashion, movies, music, or concerts we attended. There was also a lot of participation in school events, because it was really cool to do back then. Considering we had landlines and no cell phones; it was common for the corded wire to be hanging out of the bedroom door while we tried to talk privately and avoid being overheard by everyone in the household. Many parents and siblings were annoyed when they saw that cord. We had to take turns on the phone, and sometimes it was tough having to wait. Call waiting didn't become a thing until the nineties, so if the phone was in use and someone called in, they would hear a busy signal on the other end. Somehow, we managed to live through that too!

Were you a child of the eighties? What memories do you hold dear? If not the eighties, what generation did you grow up in? I'm sure every era believes that their time was the best, and teenage years the most epic. People from the sixties were hip, bold, and the grease era. The seventies were groovy, carefree, and laid back with a shared respect, curiosity, and admiration for the time periods that came before. But the truth remains: nothing quite compares to the time we lived through ourselves. That feeling can never be replicated, because it was our time. We love it, own it, and treasure it forever, raving about it as if it's ours to keep.

4
The School Playground Echo: A Letter to My Younger Me

We all leave a little part of ourselves on the playground, where we also discover who we are. Yet, it's often only later that the significance of what's been left behind becomes clear. Danielle

I took a different approach in this chapter, which challenged me a little. Writing this book has allowed me to reflect a lot, as I share many stories from the past. Now, I want to take you back in time with me to some moments from my school days. I'm approaching it as if I were writing a letter to my younger self.

I'm sure every one of us had similar experiences during our school years. Who can't relate to good and bad times on the playground, in the gym, at school dances, and so on? There were probably also many moments we'd rather not relive, like those math tests or trips to the school nurse. Some of us loved books and couldn't wait to visit the library, while others preferred the fun of gym class. Now, life is a little more complex than it was back then.

This chapter isn't just about me; I want it to be an opportunity for you to engage with your own past. As you read my letter, I encourage you to write one to yourself afterward.

Now, let's go back to the elementary or middle school yard. Let your mind wander back in time, and imagine what the scenery looked like, how things smelled, felt, and how the air flowed. So, here it is... The adult version of myself sits in my mind, looking across at young Danielle.

Dear Young Danielle,

I've been watching you on the playground, and I see how overwhelming the world might feel. You're carrying so much weight on your small shoulders, and it seems almost too much to handle. You fear being left out and feel like you don't fit in. If only I could sit next to you and talk, put my arm around you, and tell you everything I know now, all these years later.

First, I need you to understand something important: You are enough. You matter. You are worthy. Your feelings are valid. You deserve love and belonging, and even though you can't see it right now, if you keep moving forward, you'll achieve so much. I know that when you look around, it seems like others have it all together, with better clothes and cooler friends. But my sweet one, that's all an illusion. No matter how perfect they seem, they might not have it figured out any more than you do. I hear you telling yourself that you're an outsider, but don't let those words linger. You do have a place in this world.

I wish I could tell you that the things hurting your heart on the playground—the teasing or feeling excluded—won't define you. I know it may feel like the pain will never go away, but I promise, it won't last forever. I see how you're always second-guessing yourself. I know you struggle looking at groups of people and wondering if they really want you around. Your anxiety about not measuring up or being rejected feels real but trust me—you are just as important as anyone else here. Many of the people around you won't matter in the long run, but the ones who do will see and appreciate your uniqueness. They'll love you for your quirks, creativity, and kindness. You don't need to fit anyone else's mold.

Let me tell you something really special about your creativity. Ceramics will be a game-changer for you. You'll stumble into it by chance, but it will become your creative outlet and refuge. When you walk into that ceramics class, it will be the first time you feel like you truly belong. As you shape and watch the clay take form, you'll experience a sense of pride and accomplishment. And here's the best part: ceramics isn't about competing with others. It's about what you create. You'll find joy in making things that you never expected with your hands. Yes, you'll mess up sometimes, but that's okay – it's necessary. Each time you try again, you'll get better. You'll create beautiful things, and that pride will carry into other areas of your life.

I want you to look forward to those moments. Don't let fear hold you back from living the life you want. I promise, we've got this together.

Life won't necessarily become more manageable when you become an adult, and you'll face many battles. But you will carry something from these times that will give you the strength to face whatever comes your way. You'll learn that no struggle is too big to break you, and each time you ever fall, you'll rise again.

There's one important thing I want you to know: Your mom is there for you. She's been your anchor and always will be. She may not have all the answers, and it could even seem like she has her own trials, but her love will carry you through the toughest of times. I see her as your one true friend, always standing behind you, showing her support, and believing in you even when you struggle to believe in yourself.

So, keep going, young girl. You are already the person you were meant to be, but with each step, you will continue to grow more and more into your true self from within. I want you to get up every day, look in the mirror, and see someone you love staring back at you. Yes, you. That girl right there. I love you.

With love,
Future Danielle

Looking back on our experiences shows how our self-perception has evolved and reveals what truly matters. Life may not go as planned, but embracing the unexpected helps us grow and accept our true selves. In reflection, remember when we didn't have fancy book covers and used those old brown grocery paper bags instead? It took a knack to get them just right, and they became more than just protection for the textbook—they were a blank slate for our creativity.

We didn't have social media back then, so for many of us, those book covers became one of our first forms of self-expression. Some left them blank, with just the subject title written in bold black ink, while others added personal touches. People glued pictures of their favorite movie stars, showcased their love for music or sports, or created graffiti-style art that reflected their interests. And, of course, there were always those little personal details like "Mary loves Peter" or "Nick + Sarah."

The covers were mini-reveals of who we were—what we loved, valued, and were willing to share—complete with little expressions like hidden crushes or quiet passions tucked away. It was a daring yet vulnerable way to showcase ourselves, setting the stage for our journey into how we'd express ourselves in the years to come.

Regardless of all the insecurities I had as a kid, those book covers were something I could claim as my own and be proud of. That's why I included them in this chapter—to tie it back to the importance of owning our inner selves and how we show up in the world, despite the struggles.

I think it's important not to overlook how few people truly play a strong role in our lives. We often fight the hardest or clash with those who love us the most, like our parents or grandparents, because they see us beyond our bad hair days, hissy fits, and for us girls, PMS.

I didn't fully appreciate how constant my mom was in my life until much later. She kept shaping me and making me strong. The people who keep us grounded through our adolescent tornadoes deserve a trophy.

It makes me wonder—if we could truly talk to our younger selves, would we have understood the wisdom we have now? At that age, do we have the capacity to embrace what's really important ahead? As kids, we'd wander through the creek, facing missteps, falls, and scraped knees. They weren't the end of the world, just lessons. Every bump and bruise shape us. We can't dwell on them; they're part of the wisdom we gain.

Let's invite our younger selves to meet us here and remind us of what we might have forgotten. It's time to stop hiding and embrace who we truly are. Stand proud in your authenticity. Life is messy, with its highs and lows—and that's okay. Walk with confidence, allow yourself bad days, and don't question your worth. It's all part of the journey, and it's ours to own.

5

The Space She Left Behind: An Unspoken Goodbye

The bond between a mother and daughter is truly something special. You grew inside her, and that connection runs deep. A girl-mom bond is a unique, unspoken tie that goes beyond words—something beautiful and impossible to fully explain.
Danielle

My mother passed away in 2006 at the age of fifty-three after enduring a battle with lung cancer. As I watched her fight through the illness, it became one of the most challenging experiences of my life. During this gut-wrenching time, I had many moments of concern for her husband, Ed, who had been her caregiver throughout her struggle with sincere dedication. I was in my early thirties at the time, while Josh, on the brink of graduation, was twenty-one.

My mother's health issues began around the age of fifty or fifty-one, starting with complications from endometriosis. As her condition progressed, she experienced increasing pain in her side. After her cancer diagnosis, she underwent treatments for fourteen months. From the beginning of her battle until the end, I saw her brave it all the way through in a relentless way.

Thinking of how my mom coped during the greatest depths of her illness still haunts me with hurt. Reflecting on it now, she seemed to carry remarkable strength, even though I wasn't there every day to see the struggles she faced. Despite numerous treatments, her cancer continued to spread.

I wanted to believe, with all my heart, that my mother would be alright. It felt like she had so much more life left to live, and it seemed unfair that there would be no way for her to beat it after fighting with such a force of determination. When we see those we love fight cancer firsthand, there's a sense of loss that begins upon the diagnosis and all the way through it. It isn't just about their health when they are facing such a horrible disease, but it's also about pondering the life they once knew for themselves and for you. It's a devastating reality that affects countless people.

Cancer impacts the person and their loved ones, who witness the struggle and wish they could alter the course of events. The disease brings a deep, pervasive sadness, and all we can do is offer them nurturing, loyalty, and love. My hatred for cancer is profound; it is a cruel and hard-to-accept disease that leaves everyone in shock and disbelief. There's a numbing effect as you gradually come to terms with the situation, constantly aware of the time slipping away and the unfulfilled moments you thought you had more time to experience.

I spoke with Ed daily, as he was the one primarily caring for my mom. Twenty years her senior and retired, he devoted himself completely to her well-being, which I found deeply admirable. His years of commitment as a podiatrist, always helping others, naturally extended into this role. During her battle with cancer, he rose to the occasion with unwavering dedication.

Losing my mother was gut-wrenching. She is the one who gave me life and guided me through this world, and her absence left a deep void. At thirty-something, I felt somewhat selfish because I was far too young to be without her. My children were born during her lifetime, and she got to know and spend time with them. However, they are too young to remember her clearly, relying instead on stories and photos to connect with her memory. This reality only added another layer of sadness to my grief.

When we lost our mom, I often worried about my younger brother, Josh. He was an even younger age than I was. I understand how difficult it was for me, and I can only imagine the depth of his struggle. I know he, too, has had to carry a lot inside. Josh lived with Mom and Ed until about a year and a half after graduating high school, while he went to junior college. Then, he went on to college in San Francisco until he moved to San Diego to live with his Uncle Adam. Unfortunately, it was during his first semester in San Diego that our mom died (he had just transferred). It was after that Josh came back home. Being so young at the time, Josh was well-liked and popular, often busy with friends and various activities. That social engagement likely gave him some comfort and support while he processed the hardest parts of his grief. Still, the depth of our mother's loss felt especially personal for the two of us. We were her children—carried in her womb, raised by her hands, and shaped by her love. There is a sense of pride in sharing a bond with her that is unlike any other in this world.

I felt immense empathy for Ed as he was faced with and trying to handle the death of his wife of over twenty years. He went to great lengths to organize a beautiful farewell ceremony for my mom. I will always appreciate his efforts with gratefulness in a deep way. My mother's passing was deeply felt by her extended family. Each person coped in their own way, but the shared sorrow was evident. She had touched so many lives, and the weight of her absence was carried by siblings, cousins, and close friends alike.

We often witness hardships and tragedies from a distance, watching other families endure pain while quietly hoping such suffering will never touch our own lives. Wouldn't it be nice to believe we're immune to the struggle's life throws our way? But when heartache arrives—like the loss of my mother—it shatters that illusion and forever changes us. Sharing my story with the upmost honesty and vulnerability isn't easy, but I hope it opens a way to connect with others who are also dealing with their own grief. Then we all can feel a little less alone. Even a small amount of comfort or understanding can give purpose to the pain I've endured. In this shared journey of loss, we find strength together.

Every year, February 24th comes around, and I face the anniversary of her death. Without fail, it causes me to go through a whirlwind of emotions. The day is always an agonizing one for me. I am reminded of the deep sorrow I felt at the time she died. I feel like I relive those moments all over again as I go through the day. It starts with anticipation in the weeks before the anniversary. The pain of her loss still lingers. The ache of missing her is felt down in my gut, and that never entirely seems to fade. I find myself reflecting on the overwhelming grief and the ways it went on to affect my life. Each anniversary brings me into a place of melancholy, a little wistful, and longing for our shared times. It's filled with memories, both beautiful and dreadful, as I contend with the emptiness her absence has left in my heart.

I know I will never fully get over losing my mother. There's no such thing as truly moving on or completely letting go. Mom would want me to move forward, to live my best life. She wouldn't have wanted her death to cast any shadow over my future. That selflessness was a testament to who she was, and in honor of that, I strive to live in a way that would make her proud.

Have you lost your mom? Have you felt the deep heartache of knowing you won't ever see her greet you again here on earth with her smiling face? Never another hug to be had. You won't feel her hand hold yours again.

What things helped you cope with this heavy and difficult loss?

I knew it was coming, and I said my goodbyes. But I think when the moment of death hits, and they've stopped breathing... they're no longer here on this earth... we often don't fully grasp the experience for quite some time. It's as we begin walking through the aftermath that we start to become more aware that, dang it, this person is really gone. But when it's mom, it's a whole different level of grief. All the rituals and personal things we had her help with, when mom isn't there to call and share this or that with, when her advice is absent, it hurts. It can almost be paralyzing.

What do you feel is the most challenging part of grieving the loss of your mother?

For quite some time, I felt like I was walking in a trance. The people around me and the places I went to felt cloudy. This kind of loss left me feeling like I didn't know how my life could move forward without her. One moment, Mom was breathing, even if she was dying and facing the worst health situation imaginable for her. Despite time not being on her side.

I think that in losing someone, we weather the grief storm in our own unique way. To be told that someone understands isn't necessarily what we want to hear when we feel like our heart has been ripped out and taken away from us. The glimpses of that bird, butterfly, or dragonfly bring a smile and make me retreat into a quiet moment where I might have to be alone. I feel like my mom sends me signs to remind me that she is still with me. Can you relate to that?

What ways do you think are best to honor our moms? No one else in this world carried you, only her. Now we carry them.

6
More Than Mother and Child: The Friendship That Unfolded

A neat thing about my mom is that for a time she dabbled in art, paintings, quilts, and I have some of her stuff still today!

I couldn't let it end there, you know? The chapter about my mom's death. I guess that feeling of her being gone is a constant that I'll have to live with for the rest of my life. I lost her way too early. My mother was my earliest, closest, and most constant friend. Even today, though she's gone, I still depend on her in some weird unexplainable way. Now, the world might say we aren't supposed to be friends with our kids, but if we don't share some kind of friendship with them, where do they learn how to become a friend? I realize she taught me more than just how to tie my shoes or brush my hair. I was learning her style. Despite all her struggles, I was admiring her. My mom was the person I knew I wanted to be like, especially when it came to her fun side.

While so many girls were trying to be the best friend of the popular girl at school or the one with the coolest clothes, there I was, looking up to my mother. The feeling inside wasn't a desire to be like those other girls, but a deep yearning for that special kind of friendship with the woman who gave me life. She was my role model, my confidant, and the person I admired most. The connection we had was the one I cherished above all else, and with her there was contentment.

Though we are our own person, our parents play a role in shaping how we will be one day as friends to others. Kids are impressionable humans, and they take in the interactions adults have with the neighbors, extended family, or strangers walking by the house that they don't even know. It all makes an impact. We watch them more than they are aware, probably more than we ourselves even recognize. I surely took in so much of her life. I loved the moments we had alone, where we were growing in the friendship between a mother and a daughter. I knew I could trust her wholeheartedly—and be an open book with my feelings. Yes, there were boundaries in the parent-child exchange, but when I needed a sounding board, she was all ears. My mom encouraged me to enjoy life, to find my own way. She wouldn't be responsible for my happiness—and I learned that at early on. But she passed down wisdom to find happiness despite anything I might face. It was up to me to choose whether I carried it or not.

I have heard people express that 'she taught me how to do everything except live without her' when they lose their mom. That sentiment is a heavy weight when the grief is raw. While there may be some truth to that thought, I think in some weird sort of way our mothers do provide us with strength from beyond the grave before they leave us. She didn't know when her time would come. No one does. But I believe that having a great demonstration of strength instilled in me everything I needed to live without her.

Janice Salinger opened my heart with the way she loved, which gave me the ability to receive it. In return, I had it to give and share with others. She nurtured me with deep affection. Upon any disappointment or being let down by others, she reminded me to hold onto the most important things. Sometimes, letting go is actually a necessary part of love. At certain moments, it's safest for the heart to set free what it has no control over. Doing so allows healing from what it couldn't change.

Love doesn't vanish, even in the deepest darkest losses in our lives, like that of our mother. She birthed love inside my heart, which allows me to cherish, endure, and navigate grief with a courage that helps me find peace within the memory of her loss.

Mom was always showing me how to take care of the things that meant a lot—my toys, books, Barbies, etc. She taught me about resilience, responsibility, and about protecting my heart. Even in her battle with alcohol, she continued to care for me, never once letting me feel abandoned. I saw how exhaustion can weigh heavily when you're working multiple jobs yet still striving to provide for your family.

I know not everyone has a perfect upbringing, and I wouldn't say I had perfect parents by any means. However, despite everything, my mom had a certain energy that could lift those around her. No matter what she was facing, her commitment to making life better for me, my brother, and Ed was unwavering. I want my life to mirror her strength—doing my best, allowing others to be seen and heard, and being present rather than perfect.

Did my mom put too much pressure on me at times? Perhaps. But that pressure pushed me to keep going on the tough days. I never had to worry if I was safe – she always paid attention and had my back. But instead of letting life consume us she passed down emotional resilience.

My mom loved to paint, and I admired that. She taught me that engaging in hobbies could bring a part of us alive. She also presented work in a way that helped me see it not as a difficult task, but instead as an effort to provide for those we love. Because of the way she pushed me, I developed a strong sense of responsibility, especially when I thought she wasn't taking care of herself enough.

Even though I don't think she wanted me to carry any burdens, I felt compelled to support her in her struggles. My dedication to her ran so deep, I naturally felt the need to protect that strength I saw in her. My mom kept a good attitude in the face of everything. I never wanted anyone to hurt her, especially emotionally, because my sense of security was tied to hers. I think in that way, Ed was the right person for her. They gave each other something they needed.

If only everyone could all have a friend like my mom, Janice. Some people will tell you not to cross the line between a parent and friend. I think there's beauty in blending the two. Right in front of me was the perfect balance of both. Too many people today don't show the right kind of love to their kids—they see them as a chore, or something to manage. But my mother never stopped demonstrating the importance of continuous learning and personal growth. She believed that we're all learning every day, and no one is above anyone else because of job titles or status. What matters is how we handle life's challenges and what lessons we learn along the way. You can still be successful even when you don't win.

My amazing mother showed me how to have a good relationship with money, to work hard to stay in shape, and to practice gratitude, kindness, and respect with everyone. Good manners were always important to her. Even as she was dying, she remained calm and soft-spoken, showing me through her actions that we must never give up.

Mom avoided drama, believing it only caused damage and wasted energy. That's how I learned that life is too short to take everything too seriously. I often think about how she would have navigated through today's world of social media. Would we be friends on all the platforms? Of course, we would. She'd be right there, cheering me on as I fight to find my voice in this noisy world.

Mom would ask us out loud, "Why do we end up where we do?" Her answer would always be, "Because of who we choose to become." She gave me the confidence to stand strong and go against the grain, never to compare myself to other women, but to be the one who helps them fix their tiaras when they fall.

This is the friendship my mother gave me. Teaching me how to be a friend to others and then to show up for the people who mean the most to me. Who could ask for a better friend than that?

Maybe you've had a close relationship with your mom, or maybe you haven't. But let's not create comparisons. Each of our journeys is distinct, and that's what makes them special. I'm not sharing this to compare lives, but if there's one way I can keep my mom's spirit alive, it's by passing on the lessons learned by her example. If you've never known your mom, or if you've lost her, I hope to bring encouragement with these universal principles that were instilled in me about friendship. She taught me to communicate honestly, to be someone others can rely on, to have the courage to always show up, and to prioritize the people who matter most.

And, above all, she taught me that we have to love our kids enough to let them learn on their own. We can't guide them by doing everything for them or shield them from every difficulty. The balance is in letting them grow, while still being there for support. We teach them how to cope, knowing they'll need to carry those lessons on their own when we're gone-prepared, balanced, and ready for what life will bring.

It's okay to have fun and laugh with our family. Yes, even parents and kids – as a matter of fact...especially them. In fact, we should do it more often. That only leaves more funny things to share down the road. One cherished memory I have is when my mom took me to Hawaii in my teens. During that trip, I decided to get my belly button pierced. We spent time on the beach, and it wasn't until later that we realized we had stumbled upon a nude beach. The whole situation was incredibly awkward, and my mom was hilariously embarrassed. It became a story that we both laughed about for years to come, and it perfectly encapsulates the fun and close relationship we shared.

What do you love most about your mom (past or present)? Where do you feel most connected to her, emotionally, genetically, or through other bonds? Can you recall any special or funny memories that stand out? Are there unique traditions or moments you still celebrate?

Maybe you didn't have your mom or had a complicated relationship with her. Are there other women, or mentors who have influenced you in some way? Even if your relationship with your mom is estranged, the community of ladies around us plays a significant role in shaping our journey and womanhood. These women, whether through their wisdom, kindness, or guidance, help us grow in ways we might not even realize until much later in life.

Life has never been the same without my mom, but I am thankful for the time we had. No matter the circumstances, embrace the women who've touched your life, and especially cherish the friendship within those encounters.

7
Beneath the Surface: The Hidden Life of My Dad

A girl needs her dad because he's always her daddy. For the big stuff and the small stuff, for all the daddy things that matter.
Danielle

There are a lot of mixed and complex emotions when I think back to processing the loss of my dad, who was just 54 years old. At six feet two, he was boisterous and full of charm. He always presented his best side to others. Yet, despite the charisma that often outshone the struggles he kept tucked away, he would sometimes hide behind a drink, grappling with the weight of what lay underneath. When it comes to memories of my dad, I try to focus on the fun experiences, especially those shared with my stepmom Barbara (Babs) and my brothers Mikey and Matthew.

One thing that stands out in my memory is his hugs. They were warm and cuddly and captured all the goodness he had to offer.

Dad had a deep love for music, and he collected records from various genres. I remember how he and Babs would host music nights, dancing and enjoying the rhythm of life. Whenever I see some of those albums, I'm reminded of him and the joy he found in those moments.

He had a signature, Esque Cologne, which I've even ordered online to make me feel closer to him. Among his treasured possessions was an old-fashioned slot machine. This quirky piece always caught my eye and reminded me of his unique personality. I have fond recollections of childhood trips to Opryland amusement park, Gatlinburg, and the Smoky Mountains—moments filled with laughter and joy. I also remember cherished dinners at Sperry's, where he introduced me to crab legs, something I still love to this day.

A memory that stands out for me is how my dad would indulge my love for fashion and certain brands. Even though he might not have been able to afford them, he would surprise me by getting me GUESS brand apparel, among others. He did it because he knew I wanted to have those things. I would return to school feeling proud walking in style with my favorite name brands, all thanks to his generosity and his understanding of what made me feel special.

Dad loved the simple pleasures of life: swimming, tanning, and lounging by the pool. His passion for the restaurant business kept him busy. For at least a decade he often worked as a bartender. In the last ten years of his life, he transitioned into management.

I don't want to leave out someone else who was important in my dad's life. While Barbara (Babs) was incredibly good to and for my dad, their marriage didn't turn out the way everyone would have hoped, and eventually, it ended in divorce. That was really hard for all of us. After that, my dad married a younger woman named Cathy. She was really kind. I didn't get to know her all that well, but from what I remember, my brothers had a lot of respect for her and genuinely liked her. They always had positive things to say. Cathy stood by my dad through all the ups and downs and was a great support to him. I'll always be grateful for the love she had for him, no matter the challenges.

Unfortunately, Dad faced a lot of demons in his life, and it brought him to the decision that caused a self-inflicted gun wound. Miraculously, it wasn't fatal. He survived, but it was a clear sign of just how much pain he had been carrying. He was in a very manic place. We figured he had been planning out his death because he bought the gun and thought the process out when he went into the attempt. He was talking weirdly by saying things like 'God forbid anything happened to me.'

On the day he made the tragic decision to end his life, he reached out to my brothers and told them that he loved them. Nearby, an open bottle of Jack Daniels sat, serving as a painful reminder of all his struggles. It was a time marked by his inner turmoil and the heartbreaking choices that ultimately led him to that moment. The angle at which the gun was positioned left the bullet lodged behind his optical nerve, making it impossible to remove. However, it was ultimately that bullet that would lead to his death two years later.

After the incident, my dad struggled to be able to recall what happened. He experienced short-term memory loss. He would ask over and over, "What happened to me? Who shot me?" His time in the hospital was lengthy, and he struggled to remember details until the day he died. Ironically, one positive outcome of his ordeal was that he never drank or took pills; it completely changed him.

Looking back, I realize I pushed my dad away as a coping mechanism, though I still wonder if there was another way I could've handled it. After his death, we held a celebration of life at the Gold Rush Bar instead of a traditional funeral. It was heartening to see my dad's "art" side of the family—the Behars—come together, sharing stories and memories in the midst of tragedy. As we connected during that time, I was reminded of the love that remained between us all.

My dad's undiagnosed mental health struggles had a heavy impact on the relationship between us, leaving it often tangled with anger and guilt on my part. I struggled with forgiveness and coping with such a complex situation, and ultimately, I didn't see him after that tragic event, even though my brothers continued to visit him. Due to his condition, our conversations were one-sided when we talked, and he couldn't even remember my children's names.

Reflecting on his life, I often wish we had recognized his mental illness sooner, especially considering how little awareness there was about mental health at that time. We now believe he had bipolar disorder, but during his time, these issues weren't openly discussed or well understood. His family had so much hope for him to get on track and prayed he would get better. Everyone tried to show compassion and not judge what they couldn't understand. Many of them spent time reaching out chatting with him in regard to those internal struggles.

Everyone carries burdens we cannot see, and it's important to remember we never truly know what others are going through.

In Egypt, my dad was growing up in a "silver platter" world—wealthy, privileged, surrounded by cooks, servants, and every comfort imaginable. But everything changed abruptly one day when he was still young. Without warning, it was all stripped away. That kind of loss shaped him deeply and, I believe, contributed to his lifelong confusion, frustration, and sense of abandonment. I don't think he ever fully understood why hatred found its way to him or why so much struggle seemed to follow.

Looking at his life through this lens, I see how important it is to approach others with compassion. Life is rarely as simple as it appears from the outside. People often carry untold stories and scars, especially when they aren't reacting with anger or asking for help out loud. Despite everything, I still want to honor my dad and the legacies he and his family left behind. His story, like so many others, reminds me how much kindness and patience can mean—especially for those silently carrying the weight of their past.

I'm so thankful for the connections I still have within the Behar family. Staying in touch keeps a part of my dad alive within all of us, like his spirit quietly moving through our lives. My Aunt Laura, who was married to my dad's brother Ray, has been a huge part of maintaining that bond. Over the years, she's been like a family pen pal — always making the effort to stay connected. Her loving, thoughtful nature has kept the Behar side of my family close to my heart.

Have you ever lost someone tragically? It is a type of loss that shakes you to the core of your being and leaves you in a whirlwind of emotions. Grief itself is overwhelming, and with it there are so many unanswered questions left. In grief, we feel stuck and don't know how to move forward.

Have you ever dealt with someone in your life who struggled with mental illness? When you have a loved one facing mental health challenges, it can make life difficult and incredibly frustrating. It's hard to watch them suffer through a situation where you don't fully understand their pain. We may try to reach out, but they don't always open up.

How might our judging impact others? How often do we dismiss someone before we know their whole story? We have to keep an open mind and recognize that everyone faces their own battles, and not every struggle is visible on the outside.

As we reflect on this, our hearts can open to deeper compassion. My experience of tragedy with my father's mental illness later provided me with an opportunity to see myself showing kindness and understanding to others. We can honor the memories of those we love by being a guide and encouraging empathy, support, and resources on someone's journey instead of adding more complications.

8
Embracing Loss - My Journey

Loss leaves us with a pain that's almost impossible to put into words, something we can't truly understand until we're forced to face it ourselves. Danielle

To lose both of my parents before I turned the age of 40 has been an incredibly horrifying experience. The grief I've had to endure and try to adapt to is a heavy load. I've developed profound empathy for others who face similar heartache, or any form of loss. Being without parents is incredibly difficult at any age. No, I wasn't technically orphaned, but without my mom and dad, it feels very much the same. We all crave something only a parent can give—their guidance, their devotion. When we encounter moments of confusion, sadness, or disappointment, their presence is irreplaceable.

As I navigate family gatherings where my parents are absent, I often wonder what might have been. Something people will never see on the outside is how, in grief, loneliness accompanies your life. Especially during the significant milestones. There is a void there that nothing can fill. In the complexity of grief, while the rawness might fade, there's a lingering pain or ache that never completely disappears. You can even feel heartache as new realities hit you at different times. While I've watched my son, Andrew, develop a bond with some relatives in the family, it warms my heart, and he even says he wishes he could have met his grandpa Behar. When I look at my brother Josh, I notice how he carries many of my mom's traits, and I can't express how much I cherish that.

I can easily drift and think back to some of my mom's quirks. One funny thing I remember is how she would always botch up titles, which makes me smile. Audi convertibles remind me of her, as does the movie *Dirty Dancing*, which she adored. The song "You're Beautiful" by James Blunt is forever tied to her funeral day; while it's not about loss, it resonates deeply with my love for her. Similarly, certain songs from the Fine Young Cannibals quickly transport me back to memories with Dad and Babs. "Don't You Want Me" by the Human League, for some crazy reason, always brings my dad to mind.

Coping with hard memories can be so complicated, especially when I think about my unresolved feelings toward my dad. However, having my brothers by my side has strengthened our bond and kept his memory alive. Together, we have our shared grief. We've learned to acknowledge the anger and pain while recognizing that our father did the best he could. I wanted more from him, but he couldn't provide it. Still, I know he loved me in his own way.

I've come to appreciate how my relationship with my brothers has deepened due to our shared experience. Michael, Matthew, and I lost our father. As adults, we now have more in common, and I believe Dad would be happy to see the bond we share. He always wanted that for us, and it's a legacy he would want us to uphold. Josh and I lost our mom, and there's an unspoken aching silence between us, a shared understanding that doesn't need to be said aloud.

Today, I value who my parents were, embracing their strengths and flaws. If I had been able to see things from more of a bird's-eye view, I might not have focused too much on their shortcomings. With time I've come to see the beauty of their lives and who they were, imperfections and all. I wouldn't be here without them, so I owe them that.

When I hear others complain about their parents, I must admit it annoys the crap out of me. I would give anything for one more argument with my mother, for one more chance to share a moment with her. Without my parents, there's an unusual sense of something missing, and I feel a tinge of jealousy when I see my husband with his mom and dad. If Dan disagrees with his mother, I quickly urge him to make amends and visit, because life is too short, and we never know how much time we have left.

It's painful to watch others share moments with their moms, knowing I can never have that again. It can trigger sudden waves of anger or sadness, emotions I don't want to feel but do. You could say it's a reminder of what I've lost. It's hard for people to truly get it, unless they've lived it themselves.

Have you talked to someone who's helped you through your grief? Sure, we can speak with a psychologist, but if they truly don't understand our loss, the conversation can leave us unfulfilled. I've also learned that, during grief, people will often say thoughtless things because they don't fully grasp what you're going through. It's comforting to know others can relate, but grief is a journey we walk alone. My mom and dad are gone, and no one can take their place in my heart. Period.

If I could speak to them today, I would ask what they were running from and express my regret for not seeing it sooner. I wouldn't want them to ever feel that they were insufficient for me. Losing a parent is one of life's toughest challenges, and we must give ourselves grace as we step through the grief journey. It made me feel lost and alone, adrift in waves of emotion.

Have you experienced the loss of a parent? Have you lost both parents and become an orphan at a young age? We all deal with death in life, but losing a parent can reshape our entire world. How have you felt in the aftermath? It can feel as though something has stomped on you, suffocating your joy and peace. It may seem like a crucial part of our identity has been taken away.

There are countless clichés when it comes to death, and imagining life without someone we love can feel uncomfortable. We push these thoughts aside, convincing ourselves it's probably not healthy or necessary to dwell on them. But maybe if we did think about it more often, we would live differently. When a loved one dies, annoying habits or displeasing things rarely come to mind. What's remembered most are the things we loved, how their laugh sounded, how giving they were, or how they made us feel seen. Years later we often hear ourselves saying things like, "I wish I could just talk to them about this" or "I miss hearing them laugh."

Why does death seem to have a deeper hold on us when it first happens? Promises are made to live differently, be more intentional, and never to let the small stuff create distance again. But too often, old routines take over, excuses are made, time slips away, and the same patterns resurface. Then, another person dies, and the cycle repeats: vows to change, to live more fully, to be more present, and to start anew.

What erases those initial thoughts and intentions? What pulls us back into the "same old, same old" routine? The loss does have an impact, but what shifts us back to a place where the urgency of change fades, and we return to the familiar routines, even if they aren't fulfilling? How can we go from feeling so sure about our new approach to life and slip back? The intentions often diminish because we get busy and ease back into the patterns of daily life.

Maybe it's waiting through the grief process: "When this phase passes, I'll get more serious. When the next phase is behind me, I'll make those calls, host those events, spend that time." As normalcy returns, priorities shift. It's not a matter of lacking effort, but focusing on the urgency for change begins to fade until forgotten.

If you're thinking about it, don't keep it inside. Tell the people you love how you feel while you can. Ask for that selfie, write that note and send it, meet for that walk in the park, make holiday cookies, sit on the porch with that person, and chuckle over old times. It's never too late to start traditions that will create lasting memories. It doesn't matter if they seem small or insignificant now; those moments, whether complete or incomplete, will matter later. Ask yourself what you love about the people who are still here. What are the little things you'd miss if they were no longer around?

Try not to let anyone's death become a regret of things unsaid or memories unshared. It's too easy to fall into the "I wish I had…" trap. Make the time now. Say the words now. Life is too short to let those opportunities slip by. The excuses we make today often become the lessons our pain reveals tomorrow.

While we face life without those we have lost, a part of the ache may continue to burn within us. Questions arise like, "Why this? Why now? Why me?" It's only natural to feel like we've been dealt an unfair hand. Especially losing someone we never thought we would. Through time, the rawness of grief gives way to knowledge and understanding. Through my mother's cancer, I saw how illness can strike at any time. Observing my father's struggles with mental health, I grew empathy for what it's like to live with invisible agony. Maybe, in the holes left inside of us from these experiences, it carves out space for us to grow. Not just in how we understand the world, but also in how we connect with others. Being able to share our stories, we feel heard, and then also help others feel seen, heard, and less alone.

9
Blended Not Brewed: The Awkward Salinger Potluck

So, there we were, never knowing we'd end up blending together like a potluck dinner at the pavilion in the park. Yet, somehow, we all showed up with our own unique contributions to the family table. Not the original brew formula, but we somehow managed to mix and make it work. Together, we've created a cast of characters that could easily be the next big thing, with such a mix of different personalities and what we could call plot twists. So, in this chapter, I invite you into the making of the Salinger family, where connections are still being figured out. But hey, at least we've cooked up something that feels like family! Danielle

When Ed first entered the scene, I was very young and didn't understand what his role was supposed to be in my life. He felt like an outsider to me, and when he walked through the door, I found myself retreating to the corner. I wasn't ready for anyone to replace my dad, and as a little one, it was hard to understand how my mom could move on after the divorce. I was too young to fully grasp everything, but I always knew who my daddy was. I secretly hoped they might get back together, so the idea of Ed being part of our lives didn't feel great to me. He was older than my mom, and it didn't seem like the kind of fairy tale I had imagined. I guess it was something I wasn't quite ready to embrace yet.

I was too young to think about what else there was to Ed aside from his relationship with my mother. Then one day, to my surprise, I remember meeting Dan for the first time. He was facing an emergency situation after being evacuated, and his mother encouraged him to visit his dad. Dan showed up at the door, and I was immediately curious about this new person who had suddenly appeared in our lives. I became ridiculously excited, like it was a play date just for me!

Dan, who was around ten or eleven at the time, must have been surprised to walk in and find a young girl and her mother at his dad's house. I'm sure he wondered, "Who are they? Where did they come from?" He had lived with his dad until he was nine, when his parents split. As a child, he probably still held on to the hope that his mom and dad might get back together, as any child would. But there we were, standing in the way of that ever happening. In his shocked state, Dan likely felt that any hope of reconciliation had slipped even further away.

I don't know what it was, but I felt an instant connection with Dan—exciting and intense. Maybe you've felt that way before, when you meet someone and know there's something special, even if you can't quite explain it. But just as quickly as he showed up at the door, he disappeared from my life. It was quite a long time before I saw him again. But as you're aware, the story doesn't end here—there's so much more to come as you continue reading to find out what happens next with him and me in the chapters ahead.

As Ed and my mom's relationship progressed through life's inevitable ups and downs, things began to change. My mom, wanting another child, gave Ed an ultimatum. Some of their desires didn't align. Ed wasn't interested in having more kids, so he and my mom went through a split. For a brief time, I thought we wouldn't be seeing him anymore. We moved back to Nashville, and I expected my mom to stay single. But then, Ed changed his mind and decided to come back into our lives. No sooner had we settled, and I started to feel comfortable, surrounded by family, then he showed up at the door. Clearly, he loved her so much that he couldn't be without her. When he visited, there were promises of all he hoped to give her, including the chance to try for a baby. Mom and Ed decided to rekindle their relationship, and before I knew it, they didn't wait—they got married in Nashville at a Justice of the Peace. My mom found happiness, security, and the family she had always dreamed of.

The three of us then headed back to California. The back-and-forth changes were quick, and it took time to adjust. I struggled with the idea of their marriage at first, but over time, it became clear that this was a decision my mom made for herself, something I had to accept. In California, our life began with Ed and my mom. They bought a new home together, and eventually, as my mom's heart's desire was fulfilled, a new addition to the family arrived: my baby brother, Josh. My mom had always wanted more children, and Josh's birth brought her immense joy. We are ten years apart, which meant that I had to take on a more exciting role and some responsibilities of a big sister.

Ed did his best. As a podiatrist, he worked hard to provide for his family, which often kept him away from everyday moments and left him with less time for day-to-day parenting. My mom took care of Josh and me most of the time, while Ed showed his support in more subtle ways. He was the dad who tried his hardest to make it to every sports game—he'd never miss one if he could help it. But if you asked him for the score, he'd probably have no idea. (He'd show up, enthusiastically clap, and ask, "Are we winning?") But if one of his kids were sick or had an emergency, Ed was always there, ready to do whatever he could to help. He wasn't the super-hands-on, staying up with the crying baby, bouncing-a-ball-outside kind of dad, but he had his own special way of showing he cared.

Ed's parents, Eva and Loring, played a significant role in our lives, especially when it came to family traditions. I remember spending Sunday afternoons at their house in Walnut Creek.

Loring, Ed's father, was a kind gentleman. I have fond memories of him playing the organ, which I always found fascinating. He could be a bit tough, especially when it came to his lofty expectations for his children. Ed was one of four siblings: Linda, Bill, and Marilyn, who had passed away at the age of nineteen due to Ulcerative colitis. That loss deeply affected their family, and they were always grappling with it.

From what I could see, Ed's relationship with his father showed how much he wanted to make him happy. Loring had his own unique approach to pushing Ed to always give his best. It motivated him, and he decided to pursue podiatry, dedicating himself to making his father proud.

My mom had a wonderful relationship with her mother-in-law, Eva, who often shared advice on many things she was knowledgeable of. Eva also, as Ed's mom, really knew him best and was a great guide for her. It was always nice to see the strong and supportive relationship they shared.

Ed was raised in Seattle, and eventually his family settled in Oakland California. His sister Linda moved to Canada, but despite the physical distance, the family remained close-knit. Of course, the dynamic changed over the years with the passing of his parents and later his brother Bill from prostate cancer. Linda still keeps in close contact.

Ed had five children with his first wife, Joanne: Dave, Mark, Carrie, Adam, and Dan. By the time I entered the picture, they were mostly adults, except for Dan, the youngest of the five. I don't have many memories of them before Josh entered the scene, but I do recollect some moments with Mark, Carrie, and Adam. When I first came to the family after the marriage Carrie used to have me spend the night. I even remembered a trip to Chuck E. Cheese, where she worked at the time.

When Josh arrived, it was an exciting time for everyone. As the newest member of the family, he was a wonderful addition. His older siblings were in their own stages of late teens and adulthood, while Josh was just beginning to experience the world. Regardless of the age gap, Josh was always included and cherished as the youngest, a beloved part of Ed's life and new relationship for all to share.

Aaron, the youngest of Carrie's children, and Josh were born only nine months apart. Their close ages made it easy for them to bond, and they grew up more like cousins than uncle and nephew. This was around the time when I started to see more Salinger family gatherings, especially the Sunday dinners. These get-togethers provided my mom and me with more opportunities to get to know and connect with Ed's older kids.

Ed's role marked the beginning of blending his life with my mom's, which would later create a whole crew of us coming together and growing in love. Our relationship wasn't always perfect, but it was genuine. I've come to understand his love for us. I'm thankful for the support he's given me and the family we've become.

Do you relate to the dynamic of a blended family in your own life? It certainly isn't always a smooth transition. If anything, it's like trying to force pieces of a Lego set or a puzzle that don't fit. Over time, you learn as you navigate and adjust. The bonds aren't easily put together, but in the end, you see true love and connections that grow over time.

Merging families can be complex. You wonder if you fit in, who likes whom, and as you start to grow together, you move slowly so you don't fracture anything that's being built.

What do you think makes blended families work? I believe a lot of it comes down to the effort each person puts in, because we all play a part. It's about going above and beyond, seeing each other despite our differences, and navigating that icky, sticky feeling that can sometimes fill the room. Over time, the definition of what a traditional family is has changed. We don't choose our family—whether we're born into it or gain it through marriage. So, I guess we have to embrace it, right?

My brother's wife, Roxanne (whom we know as Rocky), is the perfect blend into our family. She brings warmth, kindness, and that special ingredient that makes her not just a wonderful wife to Josh, but also an incredible sister-in-law and close friend to me. I give her major props for all that she does, often behind the scenes, to keep things running smoothly for their family. She keeps me deeply involved in everything going on with their kids (my nuggets) and I absolutely love being their auntie. It's one of my greatest joys. She makes sure I feel included in the big and little moments, and that means the world to me. Josh and Rocky are my lifeline. She is a beautiful example of what it truly means to show up for family, and I'm so grateful to have her woven into the Salinger family with all of us.

10

Shining a Light on My Legacy: The Jewish Roots

The untold stories are often the most significant—the ones we rarely hear. If we could honestly listen to the stories behind the people we sit across from, whether at our own tables, workplaces, we'd be amazed at what we might discover. The stories we believe no one would understand might actually be the ones with the power to change everything. Danielle

My grandmother always said something that sticks with me: "There's nothing you can't change with a smile on your face." I carry that as a piece of wisdom, especially when I face times that are challenging. Despite any hardships that my grandparents endured, I found it remarkable how they kept a positive attitude. They didn't allow the bitterness in this world to seep into their hearts despite everything they faced. Their philosophy was that people would be people, and even though life is tough, we ultimately have a choice to stay kind, which can make all the difference.

My grandparents were Holocaust survivors. I might not share every detail with you, but it's a story of resilience, and keeping it cooped up inside is hard. When I think about how they were able to forgive and even find gratitude despite the past that they endured, it's something I see as magnificent. Many of you know how deep unspoken pain can go within our soul, and truth be told, I don't know as though I could fully grasp the depth of their ability to find forgiveness. What they've taught me is something I value. They lived their lives full of grace and dignity and showed our entire family what true humility is.

Antisemitism is a word that is used to define the hatred people have toward Jewish people. It factors into a long-rooted history with much complexity that was expanded by culture, religion, and economics. The world has experienced a lot of religious tensions throughout history. Still, I think the false accusation of the Jews even goes back to the death of Jesus, which many fuel as one of the earliest prejudices that ever existed. Society used Jews almost as a scapegoat for a lot of claims that remain baseless and only stereotypical. Hatred was misdirected and there was a maintained isolation where Jews were blamed for much of society's decline. The people who went through the Holocaust experienced something that was horrifying. It was a culmination of Nazi antisemitism that was just the start of what was to come for the prejudice in the modern age. There were so many conspiracy theories when it came to Jewish people. Unfortunately, it never really ended, and sometimes, I feel that it has become worse.

We have people in various cultures who are allowed to be extremely proud of their heritage. It would only seem fair that everyone could have the same standard. I would love to think that anything I write in my book, as I share my thoughts and experiences openly, would be understood as a part of what made me who I am today. I believe we could have a better world where everyone is celebrated for who they are, no matter their background. I often think back to when the world came together to help our brothers and sisters in Africa with their needs at that time. So many joined together on a broad scale, raised money, joined hands, and sang a song called "Hands Across America." It was people uniting together for a common purpose and the money donations were from all over the world. So how is it that, in today's world, we still see such hatred toward a group like the Jews, especially when they've made so many contributions? It saddens my heart to think that I may have to hide my Jewish identity because it could be perceived in the wrong way. I shouldn't have to fear for my life simply for standing in truth or being validated in my own identity. I want my story to be a testament to the fact that no one should have to hide who they are. No matter our heritage, everyone deserves the same opportunity to celebrate where they came from.

My grandparents had an incredible story. My grandmother and her sister were in a concentration camp, while my grandfather worked behind the scenes, delivering messages to those in the camps. He didn't have to endure the brutal treatment that many were subjected to, though he felt the immense pain of others. It was during the liberation that he and my grandmother met. Unfortunately, they both lost some of their family members in the war, but it's amazing that they found one another.

My grandparents were the prime example of heroic people. They appreciated their lives despite enduring unimaginable pain and difficulties. They had every right to be angry and resentful but chose to love and forgive. They showed me by their example how to be thankful for everything in life, including the hardships. To this day, I still find myself challenged to understand how humble they were, and that is why I embrace their story even more because I treasure it within my heart.

One person I deeply admire is my cousin Jenna, who served in the Israeli army. I have a deep admiration for the commitment to her faith and her country. I couldn't have done what she did while serving in the military—the bravery it took was incredible. She also took the strict traditions of the Orthodox faith and embraced them. Her strength, discipline, and unwavering faith continue to leave a lasting impression on me. Jenna continues to remind me of the importance of staying devoted to family, no matter the distance or the challenges life brings. I'm also grateful for my two aunts, Aunt Betty and Aunt Helen, who do their best to keep our faith and family connections strong. They keep us informed about our relatives in Israel, and we all try to support each other however we can. It's something I cherish deeply—it helps me stay connected to our customs and that meaningful part of my heritage.

By no means am I very religious, but my grandparents were, and they instilled many traditions in me that I want to keep alive. They were not just survivors; they thrived and kept moving because they believed in something greater than themselves. Because of them and the stories they told, I learned to be proud of the heritage I carry. One thing that stood out in many conversations was their loyalty to one another and to the things that truly mattered. That being said, I never saw or heard my grandparents argue. It's rare, but it's just who they were!

We have a mezuzah on our door at home, which is a symbol of my Jewish lineage. There have been times when Dan and I have considered taking it down out of fear and the desire not to offend anyone. But beyond that, it's more about keeping a symbol of safety for my family, especially my children. I don't think it's fair that I'm always in a constant balancing act, trying to juggle the world's opinions and expectations of people of the Jewish faith. No one should be persecuted simply for having Jewish blood, yet I've felt that I need to be cautious about sharing this detail with others.

I will never be ashamed of who I am. My Jewish identity is something I carry with great pride, especially because of everything my grandparents did. Though fear may linger, I choose to honor our roots and their memory above all else. I still practice rituals like lighting the Hanukkah candles and celebrating our holidays. My grandmother's candelabra, which she used to light for the Sabbath, is one of my most cherished possessions. I didn't care much about having things when she passed away, but I really wanted that candelabra, and she made sure I got it. It's a piece of my family history, a tangible reminder of all the unfathomable hardships. When I look at the candelabra, which sits in my home, it brings comfort and tears to my eyes.

Since I am being so honest, I will tell you that Dan and I had a traditional Jewish wedding. Yes, we incorporated the traditions and rituals that my grandparents held very dear. We were married under a chuppah, which, I bet many people don't know, is a symbol of the home we would be building together. We also did the breaking of the glass, danced the hora, and participated in other fun traditions. If my grandparents could endure all they did, what better way to honor their legacy than by preserving our family heritage? It's so much deeper than just the moments of tradition we practice during a ceremony. For many years, I have been hesitant in how I navigate the complexities of my Jewish ancestry and identity that I hold.

Despite all that I'm sharing, you will find me as cautious as always today. Our world is a mean place; sometimes, the most important thing is keeping our family safe. That doesn't mean I don't cherish my traditions and practice what is dear to me in my home. When I light the candles on the candelabra, I feel linked to my grandparents. But it's not just about remembering them; it's about embracing their resilience, strength, love, and forgiveness.

You could say that my grandparents were survivors who fought for their lives, family, and faith. They never lost sight of what was most important to them and somehow managed to look at the world— as dark as it seemed—with hope for a brighter tomorrow. I personally think it would take everything inside of me to reach their level of forgiveness and strength, but I will try to believe it's something I can accomplish. After all, they are a part of me, and I carry their blood inside of me, which I'm proud of. Their legacy has taught me that we can still find room to be kind, love, and forgive, even in the face of our worst enemies.

Are you proud of your family roots? Like our ancestors passed things down to us, we are passing things down to our kids and offspring. That could include food recipes, rituals, traditions, and more. Each ethnic group has unique values and practices.

Many of them are fun and come with deep meaning. It would be great to learn the stories behind these cultures. Wouldn't you love to know why some practice the customs that they do? I think a lot of them are cool. Do we realize that these legacies connect us to a different place in time? That is so profound. When you consider the way that we prepare our food in different cultures or enjoy the customs, it all ties into a big part of history. No matter what continent someone lives on, everyone came through generations that struggled and found triumph through the harder days. We are living traditions, breathing testimonies of strength and perseverance from the ones who paved the way forward so we may walk a better path. In the pieces of the puzzle, we all play a part. We carry the stories and the bloodline and have gained much wisdom from their legacies. It doesn't matter if you're European, Italian, French, Canadian, or Puerto Rican; you get my drift. Every person should be proud of who they are and where they come from.

So, how do we do better? Can we appreciate one another's culture, and the stories we can share? How do we handle this fear and division that holds us back from ever having a better tomorrow we can embrace? We are all unique individuals who can thrive together. Is this the future we want to pass on to our kids? Why wouldn't we want a better human experience for them? Is it that we want to give them struggle and fear? Or maybe we could rather help them to realize at their core they were created in their own unique way for a big purpose beyond what divides us culturally. Maybe we can start to see things through the lens of forgiveness and love. I want my children and grandchildren to celebrate their heritage. They deserve that chance to do so. May the legacies of those who came before us be allowed to live on as ones of honor. Just like I received so much from my grandparents, and what they gave continues to influence who I am today, I want the same for my kids and all the generations coming after us.

It shouldn't come down to the question of "Is everybody doing it?" We can choose a path forward, even if nobody else does. We can't wait for everyone to be on board for something like this. Every day, we can choose to be against the division, to choose to love instead of hate, and to accept instead of reject or judge others. The choices we make right now are the ones that build our future into what it is going to be. So, who is with me in getting this world to a place where we join for a better tomorrow for all?

11
Dan & Danielle: A Love Story with Extra Steps and a Salinger Twist

Love is not just knowing who you love but understanding the depth of that love – and embracing the unknowns within it. Danielle

To reestablish the context for this love story chapter, Dan and I were connected—not immediately, but through the relationship between his dad, Ed, and my mother, who eventually married. We didn't grow up together nor in a traditional blended family. Ed's marriage to Dan's mother, Joanne, didn't last, and they divorced. Later, my mother, Janice, became Ed's love interest. Their simple marriage marked the beginning of something significant: it was the thread that started to tie our families together.

For much of his teenage years, Dan and I rarely interacted. He was focused on his own life, dealing with the struggles of being a teenage boy. He was active on the school football team and spent a lot of time hanging out with his friends. It wasn't until Josh was born that Dan and I started crossing paths more often. At first, it wasn't anything significant, but over time as Dan came around more, I began to develop a crush on him—an attraction that only intensified the pull I'd felt since we first met.

As we spent more time around each other, my feelings for him began to grow. At first, Dan was an unfamiliar presence in my life. We hadn't grown up together, so it felt a bit like meeting that boy in gym class who makes your heart skip a beat—the butterflies, the lingering looks. The older I got, the more I began to understand those teenage girl feelings, and I knew I was drawn to him for reasons I couldn't quite explain. It went much further than his really good looks. He made my heart skip a beat. It felt almost like a magnetic pull from within, drawing me to him. I wanted to be around him all the time.

But then there was the taboo—would the family understand? One day, we started talking more, and it felt different—like talking to a crush. Was it weird? Nope. Not for us. Was it stupid? Not at all. We were simply getting to know each other, exploring a connection without judgment. You can't control who you develop feelings for. Your heart takes you where it needs to be.

Life is full of opinions, and we can't always control how others perceive us or our actions. People will talk, they'll try to label things that don't fit into the boxes they're comfortable with, and sometimes they'll judge us without knowing the whole story. But the truth is, no one knows the intricacies of a relationship except the two people involved. Our connection wasn't built on a traditional foundation, and maybe that's why some people might find it hard to understand. But isn't that what life is? A series of unpredictable, sometimes unexplainable moments – understood only by those living through them.

What matters is that we were two people who connected in a way that felt right for both of us, at that time. We didn't ask for the opinions of others because, honestly, their judgments weren't going to affect us. We were living in a moment that was uniquely ours, where the world's expectations didn't have a place. When you find something special, something that feels real and true, it doesn't matter what others think or say. It's your life to live, and your happiness to define.

We didn't let the opinions of others stop us from exploring a relationship that felt meaningful and worth pursuing. We aren't bound by what others believe to be "normal"—we're bound by the connection we have, the love we share, and the life we've chosen to build together. We're writing our own story. And no matter what anyone thinks, this is our journey, and we're living it the best way we know how. With caution, we wanted to take it slowly to avoid getting hurt, making sure we built something real and lasting.

Here's a funny story. Initially, when I was in high school, to keep the details of my love life to ourselves — since it wasn't the right time to share everything — I invented a fictional character from Nashville named Patrick. I felt the need to preserve what we needed to be kept private. Some of my friends found the Patrick story pretty hilarious. It gave me the perfect way to share my "adventures" without revealing the truth. I got to have my own little romance. While all the other girls were talking about their relationships, I was over here with my mysterious Nashville guy, living out my love story in stealth mode. Little did they know, "Patrick" was really Dan, and I was just keeping it under wraps for a little while!

There came a point when Dan wanted to give me the space and time to explore other experiences, so we decided to take a break for a while. Being a little younger and not having lived much of a life yet, he thought it was only fair to me. He wanted to see me have the chance to experience some adventure. We agreed to spend time apart. During that time, I dated a couple of other people. So, we each took time to explore, hoping that it would help us grow and eventually bring us back together. But unexpectedly, and unbeknownst to me, Dan met a girl and grew close to her.

My mom picked up on things long before I was ready to talk about it with her. Eventually, we reached a point where we couldn't avoid the situation any longer, and my mom knew it was time to address it with me. She pulled me aside and we sat down to talk about how serious things were getting between Dan and another girl. Mom understood the situation from both sides because she had once walked away from her own true love. She saw how their backgrounds didn't align and how she had never felt "enough" in that relationship. She also recognized how many obstacles had worked against them. That's why it mattered so much to her. Mom didn't want the same outcome for me, especially since she saw something special between Dan and me, something more than just a passing connection. Above all, she saw the way my eyes lit up when I talked about him.

But time was ticking, and things were about to change. I found myself conflicted, as I was still young and wanted to have fun, but I couldn't ignore the pull of what might be. With limited time and everything happening fast, I called Dan one day to see if I could change things. He told me that if I was serious, he would break up with his girlfriend. Was it easy for him? I'm sure it wasn't. But he made the choice without regret. I was never really sure what he said to her. Given that we were a hidden gem, and she was far away, I'm sure he explained it in a way that made sense to her. That's just how Dan is—always a gentleman. He had to put out of his mind everything that had once been between them. I was Dan's first and one true love. There was nothing worth losing what he had found with me. Then Dan and I became official once I turned eighteen. My love for Dan goes back further than I can remember. As I grew up and matured into a woman, I always had my eye on him. I believed, and still believe, that he is my soul mate.

It wasn't until I graduated that I told my friends the truth about Dan. That was when our relationship became public knowledge. We would both be heading off to college—he to finish law school and I to begin my undergraduate studies. So, the word was out. How was it received? All I can say is, it was what it was. Telling my dad and his side of the family was especially difficult because he didn't understand it. Despite the awkwardness, we kept going. It felt so freeing to express my love for Dan. We announced it proudly and with excitement.

One memory I have on our first official date, was going to San Francisco. It was there at Houlihan's, the place where I tried my first cocktail. I vividly remember enjoying the ice cream cake Snickers pie. It was a magical and memorable day. We walked, ate, and spent time at Golden Gate Park. That day officially marked the beginning of our relationship. After that, we were inseparable: walking, shopping, going to the movies, dining out, and just spending time together. We had a strong connection, and we were both committed to making it work. We had a lot to fight for—our love, our connection, and our future together.

You'll soon be reading about our wedding day in the upcoming chapters of this book, where Dan and I eventually married and began our life journey together as husband and wife in 1997. What mattered most to us was having each other. We had our love, our friendship—and that was everything. Only it was just the beginning for what would come next!!

In the times that we are living in today, how many people can say that they fell in love early and are with the one that they began their life with from a young age? Dan and I are still in love and still together. We've been married twenty-seven years. When I think about our love story, I often think of the movie *Sweet Home Alabama*. I always wanted him to be the first and last person for the many things we would and will experience. We were deeply in love from the beginning and have always had a special connection.

If you are married, how did you know your spouse was the one for you? Did you even imagine how much your life would change going from single to hitched? It's incredible to think of all the billions of people on earth how we find our 'one.' Some date for years before making a commitment, while others marry quickly, feeling like they just know.

How do we know this is the one we are ready to build forever with? Regardless of the path, we still see some marriages win and thrive forever, while others fail. If we could live in a world where divorce didn't exist, it would be amazing. But the reality is, marriage relationships are hard. It's not easy to combine two lives into one. One person alone has their issues, let alone having to adjust and get along with another as a unit. But we managed to do it. We are rocking it man!

When you think about marriage being for life, and making that commitment at a young age, it's actually kind of scary, don't you think? To grasp the idea of kissing only this one person for the rest of your life and no one else ever could be hard for some. Then you have to consider dealing with their habits, or their smelly armpits, and enjoying the highs and lows as a couple. How many people really face serious arguments during their dating years? If they do, they have probably already broken up and never thought of putting a ring on that finger.

Is it just me, or does it seem like people today don't invest as much in their new relationships to make a lasting impact? It's like they give up so easily. I honestly don't know if I'd want to be young and just starting out on the journey to find a marriage partner. Not that I think it would be scary, but today's generation is faced with so many more complexities and pressures.

Isn't it amazing to think that we actually figure this thing out? When it goes from being infatuated with their good looks or sexy smile...to feeling something beyond the butterflies and life gets real and deeper adult feelings start to settle within us. Like a bug bite that gets into our system! Now we understand when they say we've been bitten by the love bug.

12

Our Wedding Day

The wedding day is the day we marry the one who changed everything—the one who captured our hearts in a way no one else ever could. It's the day we can't wait to rush down the aisle, to stand face to face with our forever love. At that moment, we're not thinking about the challenges that may arise. We're simply living in the joy of what's right in front of us—the beautiful union of two lives becoming one. Danielle

Dan and I were married on July 13th, 1997. It was an amazing day. Our wedding featured a beautiful color theme of periwinkle and silver, and we celebrated with a romantic outdoor ceremony where we exchanged traditional vows. Before the big day, I enjoyed a wonderful bridal shower planned by my best friend Melissa in Lake Tahoe. I was pampered with thoughtful gifts, fun scavenger hunts, and playful activities. It even included some spicy erotic gifts from the Enchanted gifts line—that only added to the laughter and excitement of the day. It was a time filled with joy, love, and unforgettable memories I'll always cherish. I especially loved seeing my mom fully immersed in the games and activities—her laughter, enthusiasm, and playful spirit made everything even more special.

My mother and father walked me down the aisle and I still vividly remember the anticipation of each step as I moved toward Dan. Having both of my parents walk me was incredibly meaningful and made the moment all the more precious.

In addition to being married on one of the hottest days of the year, we were surrounded by our family and friends, who seemed to have the greatest joy for our union. That added even more love and warmth to the atmosphere. It was wonderful to have family from out of town join us for the rehearsal dinner and spend quality time with them. I love to watch our wedding video and revisit and reflect on these beautiful memories that I cherish from the greatest day of my life.

You might be curious as to how Dan proposed to me. It was on New Year's in 1996, and he chose our favorite Italian restaurant for the special moment. Being Dan's girlfriend was wonderful, but becoming his fiancée brought a whole new level of excitement. At that point, I was officially becoming his. His attractiveness and depth of his love always drew me to him, and he continuously found ways to show his affection.

After our wedding, Dan and I went to San Francisco for our honeymoon. We spent a day—or maybe a few days (who knows, the details are fuzzy)—with our aunt from New York, which was fun, but let's just say the honeymoon itself is one big event that neither of us completely recollect the same. We both remember it completely differently! You might just catch us bickering about this on some of our evening lives, when this debate will come up. We're both convinced we have the correct version of events, but honestly, neither of us can remember what actually happened! It's like we were living in two different honeymoons. I think we'll laugh and argue about it for years to come—so, get ready for that when you hear us talk about it!

We still managed to come back from that... let's call it an "adventure," and I was overjoyed to embrace my new identity as Mrs. Danielle Salinger. I was a happy, newlywed woman! But let this be a lesson to all: Jot down little notes in a journal or mark things on a calendar because, trust me, you'll want to remember the details!

The beginning of our marriage was more challenging than I had anticipated. It has often been said that the first two years are the hardest for a newly married couple, which proved true for us. I remember experiencing a period where I wondered "Oh my, did I do the right thing?" Things seemed different between us once we were married. We were building a business and everything was new. Despite this, Dan's love for me was always clear, especially in the way he looked at me. I could reflect in the photos where I was able to see a connection where he was so so so in love with me. I sometimes miss the simplicity of our dating years, as real life inevitably sets in after you walk down the aisle.

A lot of time and preparation goes into the big day's details. Between colors, themes, guest lists, invitations, attire, budget, vendor, etc., you're contending with a lot of pressures. It's so easy to get caught up in those moments that you miss thinking about what you will embark on as your future is ahead of you. So many people don't look beyond the excitement of the wedding day and fail to consider the uncertainty of what lies ahead. It's a transition from being young and single to assuming the responsibilities of adulthood and all that comes with it. Sustaining a marriage is so much more than living on love. On the days when it was most complicated, I tried to dwell upon how incredibly grateful I was to have Dan and knowing that we were building something strong and secure. I didn't make any mistake in entrusting my future to Dan, knowing that whatever we faced in the journey ahead, we could weather any storm.

Throughout our entire marriage, my favorite gift that I received from Dan would have to be the ring he gave me for our 10th anniversary. The engagement ring, while special in its own way, was a product of a time when Dan was still in law school. He had some help from a man he worked with and his father Ed to select that diamond, so it wasn't as personal as I probably had hoped.

The 10th anniversary ring was a different story. Dan truly outdid himself with this gift, selecting a top-of-the-line piece. I could see that he put a lot of care and effort into choosing it, which made it even more precious. The fact that it was personally picked out and kept as a surprise only added to its significance. I sincerely appreciated the thoughtfulness behind it—Dan didn't just go for something conventional but chose something he knew I would love. It was a beautiful reflection of both his love and our journey together, serving as a meaningful symbol of our decade of marriage.

Do you remember the day you got married? What stands out the most from that day?

It's hard to sleep the night before, knowing that the next day is one of the most important of your life. You wake up with the excitement of wanting to look perfect, even though you've already won their heart. It's your day to be cherished—full of moments to remember, pictures to take, and a celebration of the love you're sharing.

If you're not married yet and it's something in your future, what are you most looking forward to about your wedding day? It's a day we never forget, but if we could go back, we'd probably take more deep breaths, letting those moments truly sink in. We want them to last a little longer, to soak in the significance of the day. Not long after the wedding, maybe we take a honeymoon, but then reality starts to settle in—the bills and the responsibilities. At first, we're excited to handle it all together with the person we've decided to spend forever with. But then, one day, it hits you: you're now a fully grown adult, responsible for everything, managing life with the love of your life by your side.

How do people make it past twenty, forty, or even fifty years of marriage? How many of us have taken the time to sit down with the older generations, asking them to share their wisdom and experiences to understand what made their marriages last? There's so much we can learn from their journeys; from the challenges they've faced to the ways they've found to keep their love strong. How often do we seek their insight into what truly made their relationships endure? Maybe we watched them, admired the love they shared, and wished for that same kind of lasting connection. We all want that. No one walks down the aisle hoping that their marriage will end or fall apart for something "better."

When we commit to someone, we're hoping for forever. So, what is it that makes some marriages last through the decades while others don't even make it past a few years?

Maybe it comes down to the things we don't always see—the patience, the sacrifices, the times when love isn't easy, but we choose it anyway. Maybe it's about learning how to grow together rather than apart, about understanding that the highs and lows are part of the journey. There's a certain kind of resilience that comes with time, and perhaps that's the real secret to long-lasting love.

13

First Love, Then Kids

We start out as two lives becoming one, and then suddenly, we're as one making little lives together. Now how cool is that? Danielle

First comes love, then comes marriage, and then we have children. Being a wife and a mother was something I always had longed for. Wishing on a star to find that husband and have a family was so important to me. Even from a young age I always tried to imagine what it would be like to have children and it brought both excitement, as well as being a little scary. I didn't know exactly what might be ahead, but I was ready to embrace whatever the future brought for me.

When I found out I was pregnant with my first child, Jennifer, I brimmed with excitement. I had a relatively smooth pregnancy with her. Preterm labor kicked in at thirty-one weeks with her. I was on a medication to stop labor and then on bed rest until I delivered her three weeks early. It's funny, I look at a picture from that day where I can see how much of a mess I was. It was as if she just came out. There I held this beautiful little girl for the first time, and I stared in awe as I marveled at the reality she was here. It was in that moment that Jennifer made me a first-time mom.

Fortunately, all of my pregnancies were relatively easy, and I know not everyone has such a smooth experience. I gave birth to all of my children naturally and didn't have to undergo any c-sections. For Jennifer I had full medication, for Hannah I went without drugs, and for Andrew I also had medication.

Ironically, I've never had any surgeries in my life. (My children have also been fortunate in their health, never experiencing broken bones or serious injuries, despite being active in sports throughout the years)

I was spoiled by everyone with wonderful baby showers. For Jennifer, my first, I chose a vintage Winnie the Pooh theme with pastel purples. When I knew Hannah was going to be another girl, being that she was not far behind Jennifer, I continued with the same theme. For my third child Andrew, I went all out with a sports theme. Preparing for each new addition brought Dan and I great joy.

I was able to nurse all of my children and love the special bonding experience that it provided for me. Jennifer was my longest nurser, and we continued for about six months. She had her own unique routine and especially preferred to nurse at night. I still remember the last time she nursed when we were on a trip in Nashville. That marked a milestone for us while we were there. The other two, Hannah and Andrew, nursed for a shorter period of time. Once I started supplementing it helped speed up the weaning process, and they were situated at around eleven weeks. Each phase of nursing was a bonding experience, and it offered so many benefits for my little ones. I am thankful for the moments of connection and the nourishment I was able to provide to them. I recognized it could offer a significant impact on their early development and that was important to me. Because I was working as a full-time mom it was probably more inevitable that I didn't have the ability to maybe nurse as long as I would have liked.

Fortunately, I didn't experience any of the postpartum affects that can sometimes come after a pregnancy. Anything I had was more related to baby blues, primarily due to exhaustion. With Andrew, I was twenty-nine and it was more feelings of uncertainty at that phase in my life. I was a little apprehensive about facing the demands of infancy once again. It was certainly a transition, but I managed to handle it better than I had anticipated.

I worked at a daycare center, which allowed my children to be able to come to work with me during their early years. Having them with me at daycare meant they could be surrounded by a caring atmosphere and develop skills alongside their peers while being able to enjoy that mommy was nearby. It was a unique and enriching experience for all of us, combining my professional life with the joy of watching my kids grow and interact in a safe, supporting setting.

Another benefit of working at the daycare center was the opportunity to have nice big birthday party celebrations. I felt very fortunate that I could organize and celebrate these special occasions in a great work environment. I vividly remember Jennifer's first birthday party, which was a big one. All of my children had particularly memorable birthday parties where we went all out with decorations, games, and treats, which created a joyful and festive atmosphere.

The stages of childhood happen so fast and before you know it, they are all grown. I wanted the little things to last, but they go very quickly. I cherished each and every moment of the growing up years with my kids. I especially loved the simple joys like reading to them and spending quality time together. That allowed me to connect deeply with my kids while creating great memories. The time we spent doing the day-to-day things was very precious and I felt fortunate to be able to be fully present during each stage of their development.

- Motherhood and Parenting

I believe that my kids came into my life at just the right time, if such a thing exists. There are always going to be challenges and adjustments that you have to navigate when you become a parent, especially during the early years. I can see that today's parents are significantly faced with more societal pressure which can add a lot of complexities to raising children.

I would say I feel lucky in the respect that when I had my kids we lived in a different world. As parents in general, we all strive to ensure the safety of our children. We know they may be faced with bullying, as much as we hope they neither are victims or perpetrators of it. We also try to encourage them to be independent thinkers and not to follow everything the crowd says and does. I do feel a sigh of relief that my children have passed all those stages, yet I do worry some for my nieces and nephews and the challenges they may face with this new generation we are in.

Thankfully social media was not a part of my childhood, and it only began to really emerge for my kids when they were teenagers. My first experience with social media was Myspace, which certainly probably dates me. Kids in our society today struggle with communication skills, as their childhoods are increasingly dominated by the world of technology. Even my kids' lives weren't ruled by phones, but nowadays children are getting their own phones before they even reach double digits. There are many benefits to having the technology today, but I think we need to be better accustomed with how it is navigated in our lives.

There are certain fundamental lessons that should be imparted within the home rather than learned elsewhere. Core values such as love, morals, what respect is, and an understanding of healthy versus unhealthy are best taught by family. The way you are raised during your formative years can potentially have a huge impact on who you become as an adult. It influences your personal development, independence, and the way you perceive and approach various thoughts or aspects of life. The early introduction of these lessons and life skills are critical. They are the foundation for a child's future well-being and character. It is essential to ensure that these principles are instilled within the home.

It seems that today the respect for parents is less common among kids compared to back in my day. We never would have got away with some of the behaviors that are more prevalent today. For us, honoring our parents was a given. Especially on special occasions like Mother's Day. To me a perfect Mother's Day involves spending quality time with my children, my brother Josh, his wife Rocky, and my niece and nephews. Having them around creates a sense of closeness to my mom, even though she's no longer with us. These gatherings provide a meaningful way to celebrate and remember the values she imparted to us, making the day truly special and fulfilling.

When I think of the ones raising children today, I would encourage them to hang tough because it's a bumpy ride. For me, parenting was both a beautiful dream and a hard journey all in the same, with blending moments of joy, yet with significant challenges. Every parent has their own idea of what they expect, and these expectations definitely have an impact on the dynamic of a marriage and children.

I was fortunate that I had a husband who supported me wholeheartedly. He recognized and respected the role that I played, and allowed me to keep my focus where I needed it to be without becoming jealous or demanding of me. His patience and understanding was invaluable, and he didn't disrupt the relationship with our children. We were two partners who embarked on the parent journey together.

As mothers, there are numerous sacrifices to be made and sometimes we feel compelled to handle everything on our own. It's always important to remember that reaching out for help is not a sign of weakness, but actually a part of balancing the responsibilities. My husband Dan, was exceptional in this regard; he supported what I needed to fulfill in my role as a mom. Because he was willing to take a step back and let me lead where I needed to, it is only a testament to his understanding and commitment to our family's well-being.

I think that today's moms face a set of stereotypes and people are so much more critical than previous generations. Thinking back to the fifties, sixties, seventies, and even the eighties, mothers did not face the level of scrutiny and judgment that modern-day mothers now do. Every family structure has its own unique scenario. Social media just further complicates true reality and presents an unrealistic portrayal of motherhood.

While the ideal versions of family life which are depicted in shows like *Leave It To Beaver* were never truly reflective of real life, today's media often sets unattainable standards and promotes a false sense of perfection. There's an emphasis on flawless portrayals that creates unrealistic standards for mothers. It actually over shadows the genuineness of their lived experience. This makes it all the more challenging for women to feel supported and understood. It is essential that we recognize and learn to embrace the imperfection of our real life. If only it could be acknowledged that every mother's story is truly valid, deserves respect, regardless of any societal expectations, then we would live in a happier world.

One aspect of motherhood that's worth mentioning but often isn't discussed today is the use of discipline, such as spanking. It is something that is no longer considered acceptable in our society. This culture shift has for some led to moms not caring as much to deal with things. It is very frustrating and disheartening. In our time, we had a different approach to discipline, and we understood the consequences of our actions, like being corrected with a fly swatter or wooden spoon. I even recall a friend who had to choose her own punishment tool which was like a twig switch and that reflects back to the hands on approach we had for discipline. Such methods today would be considered child abuse. You look back to our generation however, and you can see that this way of life contributed to a more respectful and better behaved generation. Kids today would never understand the concept of 'wait till your father gets home.'

Most likely the absence of discipline in today's parenting landscape has led to an increase in behavioral issues and a lack of control among our children. While it may not seem so to us today, it's important to understand the historical context of discipline and how it made a great impact on behavior that provided insight and can still do so today. There could be ongoing discussions about more effective parenting practices.

As a society the importance of kids isn't as prevalent as it should be. There's a profound responsibility we have in shaping the next generation. There should be much more emphasis on the children of the future, yet it seems to have taken a backseat to more cultural priorities. It's critical as a community to do a better job in addressing this issue. The negative influence of social media has compounded existing challenges, frequently exacerbating difficulties of parenting and distorts the perception of what is normal or accepted. We have convinced ourselves that things can only get worse, but if we were to pay closer attention and make concerted efforts we could actually make significant improvements before it's too late.

As I think about my future grandchildren, or my nieces and nephews, I realize that our action or inaction will result in something that extends beyond our immediate families and future generations. If we put more focus on the needs of our children and improving the environment they are growing up in, we can work toward a future where the next generation is better supported. They may actually become more grounded individuals and be more prepared to face what's to come in this world.

It would be so great if we could get back to the basics of life in a world where practical life skills are being overlooked. It's so essential to put more importance on teaching our kids core competencies that they need for becoming adults. For example, I think about incorporating home economics back into the curriculum in the school system, teaching our kids how to manage finances, how to write in cursive for a signature on a check, and so many more invaluable life skills that they could be taught.

Children today don't present to have the coping strategies and everyday skills that they need. We cannot continue to neglect such important things. I do take pride in the fact that my children have embraced some of the traditional values. For example, my son Andrew not only knows how to read a map, but he also has a deep appreciation for classic rock music, which I find incredibly cool. The blending of old school skills and interests demonstrates the importance of getting back to the basic habits and hobbies. If we reintroduced these practical skills and timeless hobbies to our children's, we could prepare them for a more developed and well-rounded understanding that would provide for a greater future.

Mothers and fathers both have their own unique critical roles in their children's life. There are definitely aspects in parenting that only a mother can fully understand and provide, especially given the unique qualities and instincts which a woman possesses. Our ability to comfort and nurture is different than that of men. While fathers are capable of compassion, there is a distinct innate ability a mother may offer that comforts and supports their children and that sets them more into that 'motherly' role.

Motherhood has taught me that life and relationships are hard work and require constant effort because nothing comes easy. It is essential to pursue the passion of our heart and to support those we love. There's no manual with all the answers. We learn as we go.

I don't think I would do too many things differently if I could do it all over again. Maybe I would have asked Dan to be more involved with certain things, because he could have offered support when I wanted to handle things on my own. I might have coddled my children a little less while encouraging more independence. If they had been given more chores as children, there might be less confusion when asked to do something task wise today, "Wait, you want me to do what?"

No one told me how to do it, and I figured it out as I went. But I can definitely recognize the distinct difference from romantic love versus parenting. Motherhood is a love unlike any other and I can't possibly imagine experiencing life without the journey of it. I am incredibly proud of how my children have turned out despite anything we faced along the way. Dan and I are a testament that it can be done and that we live in a world where we can do better if we work together to achieve it. Despite all of our imperfections we can still raise children who are 'world ready' by the way that we shape them for their future.

Now that my children are all adults and in their own course of life, I can only hope that on this new path the value of the lessons I instilled in them will offer as a guiding light on their journey. While I may not always agree with or fully understand their decisions, I recognize that they each have their own lives to live, experiences to be made, and growth to achieve. This is their journey, and I will always be there to offer my advice and listen when they need an ear. My role has shifted now from guiding them to showing support as they navigate their own path.

Remember what it was like pushing your kids on the swing, then one day they didn't need you any longer? They get our guidance when they learn to balance on their bike and before you know it, they are riding around the block by themselves. It's our responsibility to give them the best we can. They need our guidance, our push, our support. And then, before we know it, they find their own way—learning to stand on their own, no longer needing that push as much.

The key is just trying to balance giving them the independent freedom to grow while still being there when they need us. It's amazing to see our children begin as an extension of us, yet though they may share parts of who we are, they carve their own path and bring something entirely original to this world.

14

The Story Deepens and Endures

People often think of marriage as a relationship between two people. It's actually a place—a living space where two individuals come together to build something deeper than themselves. It goes far beyond physically painting walls or hanging pictures, but something far more meaningful is happening. You're decorating a life together, your hearts become shaped differently as your strengths, weaknesses, dreams, and fears come into the mix. It's a place where, through vulnerability and trust, you create emotional security with one another. Danielle

Looking back at our marriage and the life that we've built, has it been without problems and challenges? Absolutely not. We've had to be adaptable. In the beginning, Dan was focused on launching his own law firm, which eventually evolved into a partnership. Marriage is a huge learning curve, and you'll constantly discover new things about your partner you never knew. That happens regardless of how well you think you know someone or how long you are married to them.

Dan has always been a hard worker, no question about it. While I took on the traditional role of the wife, I was somewhat naive and insecure. I knew it was to be a partnership. Still, somewhere along the line, I had myself believing that it was my sole responsibility to care for my family and manage the house. There were times when I felt like I was living in the background. By taking on all the responsibilities, I allowed Dan the freedom to act more independently. Eventually, I had to learn to care for myself and not rely solely on him for what I needed at home beyond my monetary needs.

We have had tough times in the seasons of life and the marriage scene. We once shared the same space in a literal sense, but I asked myself, "Wasn't living under the same roof, at the exact address to be more than just managing daily routines and navigating what comes at us each day?" Living that way masked a profound distance between us. The moments we shared were mundane, as the emotional connection we once had seemed to be slipping. Sometimes, I felt pushed away and had to handle so much alone. Dan had quite a different perspective from mine and may have seen himself as the slighted one. I couldn't entirely understand that when I was feeling more overlooked. But truth be told, we were both just busy doing what was needed for our family and keeping things afloat.

We never lost our spark, but at times, things dimmed somewhat along the way. I've always strived to better myself for the sake of our relationship. Honestly, the things you used to do lessen as you go along. The little gestures that once made our connection special are experienced much less. The nature of romance can shift as we age. We tend to be more charming when love is fresh and new in those early days. After all, we need to capture the heart of the object our affection. I remember how Dan used to bring me flowers, hold my hand, and open doors for me. His romantic gestures definitely were love arrows to my heart. But over time, things changed. As we grow older, our energy dissipates, altering how we express our love.

I'd rather share this life with no one in the whole universe besides Dan. It's important to recognize that everyone has their makeup and will have their own distinct way of reacting to things. It's essential to keep working on your relationship through the trials and stagnant times while prioritizing the significance of what you are together. Being honest about your feelings and expressing what matters to you is imperative. People invest their time in what is most important to them. So, we must be aware and intentional about nurturing our marriage relationship priorities.

When Dan and I look around, it's impressive to us that many of our friends who got married way back when are still with their original partners. It's a testament to the strong family values in our circle. We place more importance on the deeper aspects of our relationships than just surface-level concerns.

Everyone has their own issues and gripes about their partner but looking beyond each other's faults is key. Nowadays, divorce seems too easy. Loyalty and trust are hard to come by, which is crucial. Every marriage has its challenges—simple things like leaving a mess to clean in the kitchen, not changing the toilet paper roll, or forgetting to buy more toothpaste before the tube is empty. The more challenging times come with financial decisions, parenting disagreements, unfulfilled expectations over various areas of romance, or countless other topics that could be named. People give up too quickly and aren't willing to put in the necessary effort. We've always been committed to doing what it takes to keep our love alive and to stay together.

At the end of the day, I cherish being Daniel Salinger's wife—even if he's difficult... just as I can be! This girl asks herself every day what 'I' need to work on to better our marriage. Successful relationships require both parties to put in a shared effort. Who's to say my way or his is the right way? For instance, if I prefer tasks to be completed immediately, I might not always need to be responsible for managing every detail. While I believe in the importance of cleaning as I go, others may have different habits and priorities. I've read the self-help books that often suggest that if you have a problem with it, it may be just that - a you problem. It's important to understand that what might be a pressing need for me, may not affect Dan similarly. Yelling at him for not meeting my expectations only creates conflict rather than fostering understanding. Recognizing and respecting each other's differences is helpful to constructively addressing these issues.

A lack of patience can become an issue when one person seeks immediate action. At the same time, the other person may not share the same urgency. Suppose I'm adamant about having something done right away, and it's bothering me more than it does him. In that case, the underlying problem often lies in how we handle our differences. Yelling and jumping to conclusions will only hinder us and not allow us to move on from a temporary upset. I need to focus and listen to what the other person is saying. The last thing I would want to do is react impulsively, possibly causing more turmoil.

I've learned with Dan over time, that agreeing to disagree on many issues is often necessary. We frequently use phrases like, "I can see what you're saying, but..." This approach has often helped us move past arguments and find common ground. We take great pride in having been together for over 30 years, with something that is timeless and priceless!

In any relationship, if and we hold grudges it can be detrimental. I've found it helpful to take a moment to process my feelings, allowing myself to reflect on and grow from the experience. Self-awareness about my tone, expressions, and overall demeanor is crucial. By taking ownership of my reactions, I contribute positively to resolving conflicts rather than exacerbating them.

So, what defines quality in a marriage? Quality time is key, but it's about more than just spending time together. It doesn't have to be sexual, either. Whether we're cozy somewhere watching a movie, handling things with Ed or the kids, enjoying dinner, or maybe a ride in the car, quality time goes farther than specific activities.

It's also about the subtle moments that express love without a word being said. Simple gestures, like touching arms or feet while sitting together or lying on the bed, can speak volumes. These little loving exchanges can convey "I love you dear" in a more profound way all by themselves to reiterate and reinforce the bond between us. Quality in marriage can be discovered and rediscovered in those everyday moments of companionship, which strengthen our relationship in both big and small ways.

Our experiences together hold an element of fun. Phrases we share among ourselves (that only we know), also bonds us differently with something that is all our own. The years and chapters of our life together have come with changes, but we have our own special kind of story, and that is pretty cool. It was a young love where we took a risk and made it work.

Our journey could have gone a different way, but here we are with our love story standing strong. I envision us in our seventies and reaching that 50th anniversary. I want that milestone to reflect the quiet strength of our enduring bond. I remember my grandparents when they celebrated their 50-year celebration. As I watched my wedding video, I was honored to remember that my grandmother wore the same dress from their own anniversary party to our celebration. It added an extra touch of sentiment to our special day. Dan is an inseparable part of my life that I can't escape. It would be so fulfilling to hear our kids say they want what mom and dad have had. I can only hope that our children will reflect on our relationship and aspire to build something similar in their lives with their partners.

How do we truly know we're compatible with someone? Do you think it is normal to have doubts along the way? I think the excitement of a new relationship can sometimes overshadow the reality of it if we rush in too fast. Yet, can someone really know, within just two weeks, that they can't imagine their life without this person? I suppose it's possible. But I think there's a difference between the early thrill and the deeper connection that comes with time. When that initial excitement fades, what are we left with? That's when the true compatibility begins to show itself.

When do we become truly certain about our person? I believe it's when our partner begins to teach us new things about ourselves. We go from wondering about who we are to being more certain of it. We've probably all experienced falling for someone before our spouse or at least had other relationships that taught us some things. But what is it about this person that makes them different from all the rest? I think it's about approaching them with fresh eyes, free of comparisons to anyone else from our past. It's about embracing the uniqueness of the connection we're building, rather than trying to measure it against old relationships.

Marriage isn't easy. We all have needs and wants, and they often change over time as we go through different stages of life. It's important to keep that in mind to communicate these things with our partners. We can't rely on mind reading—whether it's assuming we know what they're thinking or expecting them to know what we need without saying it. We are only asking for misunderstandings to arise when we don't express ourselves clearly. No matter how long we've been married, or how well we think we know our partner, there's always something new to discover about them. And that's what makes marriage so magical. Even with all the stuff, with Dan our years together have been everything I could have hoped for and more.

15

Pieces of Ed: Through the Fog: Navigating Dementia with Ed

Fun Fact: Did you know that Ed played the Trumpet for the military band? He still has his trumpet.

The signs that Ed was entering a new reality with dementia were pretty noticeable. At first, it was simple things: he'd forget how to go home or get confused about aspects of driving, frequently missing red lights and stop signs. At times, he'd even get lost in his own community. People noticed. Falls became more common, leaving him vulnerable and raising urgent questions about how to move forward. Each day, as his mental state remained unpredictable, we found ourselves navigating his confusion and the uncertainty of what would come next.

There's an initial shock or denial that comes with dementia. Despite the abundance of resources available, it's hard to find genuine guidance for coping with the emotional toll. Families often feel lost and overwhelmed, struggling with unpredictability. There's a pressing urgency to quickly shift focus to practical matters like care plans, legal matters, and daily routines. This leaves very little space to acknowledge personal feelings of mourning someone you once knew. It's like grieving someone who is still here, but different from how you once knew them.

As Ed's health began to deteriorate, it was clear he needed someone with him around the clock. Initially Mark stepped up, and Ed moved in with him full time. Tough decisions had to be made, like selling his house, car, and many belongings. Despite the challenges, we reassured him as best we could. Remarkably, he adapted without much complaint.

As circumstances shifted for Mark, it created a need for additional support with care giving responsibilities. Dan and I discussed it, and his plea weighed heavily on me. He was deeply committed to keeping his father close to family. While I was initially resistant, I understood Dan's desire and didn't want to seem unsympathetic. Ed had always been a part of my life, despite our difficult past. I couldn't allow that to factor into our decision moving forward. We agreed that the decision was inevitable.

At first, caregiving was part-time for us since Mark needed breaks due to his own situation. But as Ed's condition worsened, it became clear that more stability was needed. So, a decision was made for him to move in with us full-time. Transitioning between two homes proved challenging, as there were times of comfort at Mark's, only to come back to us shortly after.

Caring for a loved one with dementia is overwhelming, daunting, and emotionally taxing, especially in the early stages. We had to face it head-on, with no magical solution in sight. Embracing this life change was necessary, as leaving it for someone else simply wasn't an option. The hardest part is knowing that this situation will worsen over time and never improve.

The adjustment wasn't easy by any means. In the midst of all the uncertainty, it suddenly hit me: the weight of this responsibility was on our shoulders. We were right in the thick of it. At first, I struggled with denial and found it hard to summon the compassion needed to care for him. But over time, something shifted. Engaging with others on social media about caregiving opened my eyes and changed my perspective. I found people who could relate to what we were experiencing. Dan and I also became a source of support and encouragement for others. I began to see Ed in a new light and realized I could genuinely care for him. As he softened, so did I, and together we began to navigate a new chapter, growing closer in the process. I realized I could actually love this guy.

Ed, who had been a lighthearted person in his own way, was changing before our eyes. He had little peace, constantly asking questions, seeking reassurance, and expressing his curiosity.

A lot of people who go through this have certain mechanisms that work for them, but that is not realistic for everyone in the same situation. We know Ed well, and certain aspects of his personality have remained unchanged. He has specific preferences for his surroundings that bring him comfort, even despite this disease. For example, continually introducing unfamiliar people into his space would be very unsettling. He did enjoy sorting some socks at one time, but that was short-lived. He has no interest in puzzles or building blocks, and I know many people with this disease are entertained for quite some time that way. We would love that to be an option, but it's not in our case.

Critics may not understand or agree with how we do things, but we share our journey to show what works for us. We're fortunate to care for Ed at home, rather than place him elsewhere. If he were in another setting, he would likely be medicated, which we find hard to accept unless absolutely necessary. We're already seeing him lose his independence, and it's clear he doesn't fully understand what's happening to him.

Looking back at old videos, his decline becomes even more apparent. It's heartbreaking to watch. While we witness his condition every day, the recordings offer a clearer picture of how his health has gradually changed. At times, Ed will fixate on his brother Bill for days, or even a week, before moving on to something else. This hyperfocus is consistent, but every ten minutes or so, he forgets and asks the same questions: 'Where is my brother? My checkbook? Is that my car? Where is my phone?

It's quite profound how dementia affects the brain, particularly in how it distorts the recognition of loved ones. In Ed's case, this is seen in his confusion between his son, Josh, and grandson, Wesley. The disease blurs the lines between past and present in a way that is especially challenging for someone who has lived a full life and cherished strong family connections.

As the youngest of Ed's children, Josh holds a special place in his memory. The condition has frozen time, causing Ed to see him as the boy he remembers from earlier, clearer days, rather than the man he is today. This ambiguity deepens when Ed sees Josh's son, Wesley, who looks exactly like his father at that age. The visual resemblance often causes Ed to mix up the two.

In different stages of dementia, people tend to latch onto long-term memories, while recent events fade. Ed's connection to Josh is grounded in those earlier memories, but as the disease progresses, those recollections become more distorted, trapping him in a past that no longer reflects the present.

To help you understand Ed's concerns about his son Mark and Bill, they are rooted in his subconscious memories of their past struggles. Mark was injured in a mudslide when he was younger, and Ed remembers that. He was also always used to helping his younger brother, Bill, and providing guidance to him. Ed clings to these moments, especially those tied to more negative experiences. While his memory is fading, these older encounters—especially those involving who he cared for—still dominate his thoughts.

This can reveal the bittersweet nature of Ed's role as a beloved podiatrist and grandpa. Dementia is harsh, and the confusion it causes can feel even more cruel. It steals pieces of a person. Yet, it also reveals how deeply Ed treasures his family. Though his confusion can be overwhelming, our desire to protect him remains unwavering. That instinct only grows stronger as we watch his gradual decline.

Have you experienced a loved one diagnosed with dementia? Do you ever feel it's too late to do the things you wish you could have done? So many questions linger in our minds, constantly reminding us of the complexities with loss and love. Accepting this challenge in the face of such a relentless condition is heartbreakingly difficult. As the disease progresses, it becomes a process of letting go of familiar memories and the essence of who someone once was as they slowly change. We continue to find small ways to connect, adapt to new routines, and celebrate any moment that reminds us of the significance of who he was, and always will be.

Do you take time to consider your own mental health while caring for a loved one with dementia? It's easy for those caring for someone with this disease to forget their own well-being in the midst of constant care. While it's important to provide comfort for our loved ones, it can also be overwhelming because we never know exactly what to expect, and everyone's dementia journey is different.

Do you ever struggle with getting it right? There's no perfect guidebook for handling dementia—only the understanding that we must preserve what we can in the person and the time they have left. Some people live with cognitive decline for many years, while others don't last long after being diagnosed. We need to offer grace to both the person with dementia, and to ourselves. Everyone needs encouragement.

Caregiver support is vital too. It's important to have someone that you can talk to, so that you're not carrying the burden alone. It takes a mental toll. Remember that even though there are aspects about the person that are altered with a dementia diagnosis, they are still who they are. We can't forget the impact these individuals have had on our lives or the love they've given. There is still life remaining, and it should be lived in the most meaningful ways possible. We might not find any escape from the difficulty, but we can find the strength to be the support needed, ensuring everything is covered.

16
The Ed-ventures of Caregiving: Ed-ucating Ourselves Through Colliding Hardships, Hilarity, and Heartfelt Moments

There is nothing practical about caregiving—nothing easy, and seemingly nothing to be gained. Yet, at the same time, you gain so much that is useful in the process—patience, strength, and inner resilience that transforms everyday challenges into moments of growth. These lessons can't be measured by tasks completed, but are felt in the heart and mind, enriching your life in ways you never expected. Danielle

Caregiving comes with many misconceptions. When people hear the word "caregiving," it's interesting to hear what they think it involves. There are many aspects to it regardless of the type. We care for our children in their early years, for people who've had accidents or undergone surgery and need temporary assistance, for those with disabilities, and, as in our case, for the elderly. Sometimes these responsibilities are handled by professionals and medical personnel, while other times, family members or close friends take on the role.

So, what exactly is involved? It's not just about handling the needs of a person in a wheelchair or someone who is bed bound. Not everyone faces physical limitations—sometimes, like in our case, it's a mental or cognitive issue that makes it difficult for someone to care for themselves. When you're a caregiver, you take on a wide range of tasks to help meet the daily needs of the person you're caring for. This could be anything and everything from assisting daily with dressing and bathing them, assisting with housework, helping with mobility, preparing meals, dispensing medications, communicating with necessary people, and even helping to get them walking or moving around. In simple terms, caregiving is about providing the support and care needed to ensure their well-being, day in and day out.

In our case, when we decided to care for Ed, it didn't come with a set timeline or specific rules. When he moved in with us, we agreed to help with his practical needs first, then deal with more complex ones as they would arise. We've been fortunate that Ed has remained fairly mobile, but his needs, both physical and emotional, require ongoing assistance. Ed cannot go out grocery shopping, so we handle getting him everything he needs at the store, driving him to his appointments, and making sure his living environment is something he understands.

Initially, when Ed moved in, two of our kids were still living at home, which created a needed adjustment for everyone. They were capable of taking care of themselves but also had to acclimate to the new dynamic. While they loved seeing Grandpa, it was different when trying to concentrate on homework and Ed kept asking the same questions over and over. You do your best to be patient and present, while also recognizing the importance of taking a little time to recharge. It was difficult because Ed did not understand the concept of giving people personal space. Some of the social cues became harder for us, and there were triggers everywhere. The constant repetition and loss of privacy made life feel different. We tried to juggle everything the best we could. Dan had recovered from his heart attack, and while our health was good overall, the main focus started to shift more toward Ed's needs.

There are many things you don't anticipate when your home becomes the land of live-in caregiving! We no longer have the spontaneity we once did. As a couple, intimacy had to take a backseat. If we do get a moment, it feels rushed. It's like when the kids were little and you had to hurry through private moments because you didn't want them to come into the room. You never know when you will get that kind of alone time again. Constantly having to listen for Ed to possibly come through the door of our room isn't something we thought about when he moved in.

When you have a guest stay for an extended period, they may stay for a week or even a month. There are moments that you enjoy, but then there is also a normalcy that you miss. However, the timeline is very different when you move someone in permanently to care for them. You are pulled in a lot of directions, for an indefinite period of time.

When Ed came to live with us, Dan and I were at the point of living a fairly simple life. Of course, we had our family moments and events, like going to our daughter's soccer games. We were no longer living the party life, and had settled in to only occasional outings, yet still had the freedom to come and go. I was still handling the full plate of household responsibilities, managing the bills, taking care of what the kids needed (college arrangements, etc.), doing laundry, errands, keeping up with the yard, the pets, and everything else that goes with living!

Throughout this process, Dan and I have both realized the importance of self-care and making it a priority. We've found a system of taking turns to maintain our mental health and well-being. For Dan, that means taking his walks, maybe writing some of his poems, or preparing his social media content.

To stay intact amid the relentless demands of caregiving, I rely on various coping strategies. Getting up early to exercise, reading, going to the casino, having a glass of wine, and taking occasional mini trips provide necessary escapes. It helps to ensure that we can continue providing the best care for Ed.

I wouldn't say that being caregivers has changed who we are as parents, especially since our children are older and self-sufficient now. It might have had a different impact if they were younger. The role has caused me to become more independent and rely less on Dan. I don't mean this in a negative way, and I suppose this change has had its positives. But it's something anyone should consider before taking on the responsibility of caregiving.

Ed's forgetfulness and hearing loss make caregiving a daily challenge. He forgets things easily—one minute he's looking for his keys, the next he's forgotten he's already eaten cookies and wants more. The unpredictability is constant. There's no way to predict when he'll get up at night, trying to get through the gate or come into our room. It's a constant responsibility with no real rest break, and we can't delegate it to anyone else.

Everyone's caregiving journey is different. Some are dealing with less difficult situations, while others face more challenging circumstances. While this perspective helps, it doesn't change the emotional and physical toll that caregiving has taken on us. I'm also navigating the pressures of aging myself, with the challenges that come with being a 50-year-old woman. At times, the situation can feel intense. That's why I'm so grateful for my social media outlet—it provides me with a much-needed escape. If I'm being honest, I'm not sure I'd be getting through things as well without it.

What I am sharing is about transparency, I'm not complaining. I'm trying to give anyone looking from the outside a better idea of what caregiving really involves. It's something that unless you experience firsthand, you have no idea what it details. In many ways, caring for someone with dementia is even harder than raising young children. Ultimately, we were the ones that made the choice to take on this responsibility, and we own that decision.

Being that I have been through some significant grief in my life, I can say it feels like caregiving has been harder than grief. You're dealing with something that will only worsen with time. All your moments are accounted for, and there's little room for anything unrelated to caregiving. It is always in the scope of things in your life.

Caregiving has its rewarding moments of unexpected joy. It's not about receiving thanks or any recognition. It's more about knowing that we've stuck with our commitment and haven't backed down. If Ed were in a facility, it would be harder for him, and for us too. We do not regret our decision, even on the tough days.

Are you on a caregiving journey? Do you relate to what I'm saying? Is this something that might be in your future, with your parents or someone you love? Caregivers are a special breed of people, and I'm not saying this to toot our own horns—it truly takes unique individuals to take on this type of responsibility. You can't expect to be thanked, and that can be hard to handle, right? But we cope through it, because of love—because of the love we have for the person we're caring for.

This leads me to an important point – what can people do to help caregivers? Based on the experience we've had, even the smallest gesture can make a big difference. Offering to bring or make dinner, visiting Ed and saying, "I'm here for the next couple of hours, take a break," can mean so much. I'd love to have the chance to take an extra nap or even run to the casino for a little while. For example, with Ed, he really enjoys company, so if someone like his son Mark comes to visit him it is a real treat.

Now that we have been living this experience, I have had conversations with my kids about my wishes for later in life. I personally do not want them to care for me when I am older. I want them to live their own lives and focus on their families. We did a lot for them when they were young, but there's no obligation to "pay us back."

With us personally one of the things that makes it all worthwhile is that Ed is incredibly grateful, constantly thanking us for something. His gratitude toward us has made it a bit easier for us to manage, knowing that we are fulfilling his wishes. Every day is filled with moments that can be challenging, but we also have those precious moments where we see him laugh, smile, and truly enjoy life right here with us.

The love and compassion I developed while raising my children continues to shape the relationships I have today, Including the one with my father-in-law Ed.

When I assist him with tasks such as showering, the empathy I cultivated during my time as a mother comes into play. This experience helps me understand the kind of compassion and patience he needs, especially given that these tasks can be complicated for both of us. The lessons I learned from nurturing and caring for my kids now guide me in providing thoughtful and gentle support to other loved ones. It allows me to demonstrate the skills (like patience, understanding, and love) I developed in motherhood and all those things can profoundly impact other aspects of our lives.

The bottom line is that caregiving is incredibly difficult, and I've tried to share the reality of what it's like for us. For those who claim they never get tired or always keep their cool, they're likely not being honest. The truth is, caregiving is a challenging task, and the emotional and physical toll is very real. That said, as difficult as it is, it's all worth it. When we commit to caring for the people we love, there's nothing greater. There's a deep sense of fulfillment in knowing that you did everything you could, even when no one else could fully understand. I believe that when this chapter of our lives is over, we will miss it.

17

Women With Defining Influence

A woman of influence in another woman's life plays a significant role. She ignites something from within. Her wisdom and qualities stand out, inspiring others to be more like her or embody certain aspects of who she is. A woman who influences us doesn't necessarily raise us; sometimes, it's simply by being a living example that amplifies a belief—that we can love deeply, grow, and transform into the best version of ourselves. She offers us her baton to acknowledge that we are capable and the things we desire the most can be within our reach. Danielle

When it comes to women of influence, I have had two phenomenal ladies in my life that I was able to call my own. My mom and my bonus mom. My birth mother shaped me from childhood and will forever hold a high place in my heart. From the time I was a little girl, she always picked me up when I was broken or sad. Her love was unwavering and unconditional. Though she's no longer here, I feel obligated to honor her. Each day, I push forward. I have always been determined to live out the strength and self-worth she instilled in me. It can be complex and conflicting sometimes because she's been gone for so long, and I wonder how things might have been different if she were still alive. I miss her deeply, not just for the love she gave but for the guidance and comfort I no longer have. I can only reflect on memories now.

My mom faced a lot of conflict in her life, yet she taught me so much through all the challenges. I always admired her bravery—how she left behind the stress and struggles in Tennessee, creating a better life for herself and teaching me to value myself. She showed me that it was possible to rise above the misguidance and losses she faced. Despite any of her faults (which we all have), she is someone I will always be proud of. She wasn't just my mother; she was my champion and lived a demonstration of what perseverance looked like, even when the odds were stacked against her.

It's strange and a bit overwhelming to realize that I'm now at the same age my mom was when she began her cancer journey. It makes me reflect on the path I'm walking and how the lessons she left behind continues to guide me. If someone were to ask me at a younger age if I had the same outlook on her influence that I do now, I probably wouldn't. Her impact has deepened with time, especially since her passing. It's true what they say—you appreciate people more when they become a loss. Now, I see more clearly the strength she carried, the battles she fought, and the depth of her love, even if I didn't fully understand it then.

Another woman who greatly influenced my life was my stepmother, Barbara—whom we affectionately call Babs. She remains a part of my life today and still checks in on me and my family. Even with bringing something entirely different to the table than my mom, I now realize I needed both of them and their unique qualities. My life was chaotic when Babs came into it—I was around nine years old. She's always at the top of my list when I think of incredible women. Babs played a key role in keeping my dad accountable for maintaining a relationship with me, and for that, I'll always be deeply grateful. She was young, carefree, and always seemed at peace—exactly what I needed at the time. In the middle of all the noise, her calm, unbothered presence offered a kind of perspective I didn't even know I was craving.

We even found joy in simple things, like clipping coupons together, which somehow became fun because of her light-hearted nature. I remember watching her take care of my dad, even down to clipping his toenails, which I found a little strange but also a reflection of how much she loved him, even when he struggled with alcohol and pills. She was chic and patient, making countless sacrifices along the way. Over time, though, she realized it was necessary for everyone's well-being to take a step in a new direction—a path that would offer more peace and stability for herself and my brothers.

Looking back, I understand her pivot. She took the reins and raised her boys as a single mom when things became too much to bear. I admired her strength and grace, even through tough times. Babs showed me that love is powerful, but sometimes, protecting yourself and your family requires making hard decisions. What stands out to me the most is that, despite everything, she didn't bring anyone else into her life while raising my brothers. She waited until they were grown and graduated before she started dating again, which I respected deeply.

If I could say one thing to my mom today, I would say "I love you, and I appreciate everything you did." She is the one who taught me how to navigate life, be resilient, and always aim for something better. When the odds were against us, it never became a factor for her. Her life was molded by her parents, immigrants who survived the toughest of times, and that survivor mentality was passed down to me, ensuring that I would rise above whatever limitations were placed on me.

I was fortunate to have these two incredible women. Though they were very different, both brought something invaluable to my upbringing. My mom found joy in her home, children, and grandkids. She was resilient and determined, teaching me to be independent and never rely on anyone, especially a man. Nothing is ever guaranteed, and my mom instilled in me the importance of education, self-sufficiency, and taking care of myself—like seeing the dentist every six months. Babs showed me patience, calmness, and how to find peace amid chaos. Both were working through their own challenges, but in doing so, they gave me what I needed to grow.

I honor both my mom and Babs for their roles in my life. There was something in the way they parented and loved their kids—the sense of pride I saw in their eyes when they looked at us. It gave me a deep sense of something that lingers to this day, and I knew I wanted to be a mom like them someday. Their impact helped me set things straight and gave me a compass – not just to stand on my own in the face of adversity, but to love, lead and steer my own course.

With that in mind, here are some things to think about:

"What is an influence?"

With me, it was a lot of guiding and teaching by my mom and Babs, and it inspired me. Whether through what we believe or how we behave, but in a way that is not too forceful. It all leaves an imprint in our hearts.

Who were the women in your life who helped shape you, and in what ways? Why is influence important?

Reflecting on the ways we've been guided positively offers insightful perspectives. We can be enlightened during tough times through the wisdom of others' experiences. Don't take for granted the gift of having solid people to look up to or forget that many others are surrounded by negative influences. Those who model bad habits by dismissing, undermining, or belittling the goals and achievements of others can be a destructive force. That's why I'm especially grateful for the grounded, stable women I've had in my life.

"Who do you influence?"

We all have people watching our walk. It could be our children, family members, friends, or even neighbors. If we are connected to people on social media, we have a certain degree of influence on what we post or how we respond to things. Some people see me as an influencer through my social media. I love to share lessons I have learned on resilience and empowerment to help people become more vigorous.

I pass on my values about allowing people to see themselves as valuable, worthy, capable, and independent. Using my match, I hope to ignite the sparks for others to feel brave and follow their path with unstoppable determination. Discussions can arise in various settings—whether with my Zoomies, during my morning workout livestream, when Dan and I are live, or with my membership subscribers—where we have the opportunity to offer advice and be a steady presence in the lives of others. It's in the small things, like listening or responding when somebody is going through something that is hurting them. I want to believe that every day, I strived to provide some hope or made a difference in another person's life for the better. Just like my mom and Babs did for me.

18

The Power of Every Step: Danielle, Leading With Every Treadmill Stride

There's power in every step we take, every bad decision we pretend we didn't make, every troll we ignore (until we don't), and every day we wake up and think, 'Well, here we go again.' Danielle

I would never boast, but I sorta kinda believe I bring something distinct to the digital landscape. I'm more than just Ed's daughter-in-law or Dan's wife. Sure, I've got some family ties that might be considered noteworthy—my uncle played for the Jaguars, my aunt married a member of the music group Berlin, and Dan has ties to the legendary writer J.D. Salinger. But beyond all that, I've carved out my own space, my own voice, in the ever-evolving realm of social media.

I don't consider myself merely an influencer; I'm also a passionate advocate for caregivers and women. When Dan initially suggested that I trust the process, I never anticipated any fame would follow. My journey began with a simple video about dealing with a lock on the pantry door. After Dan's heart attack, he stepped back from his firm to do more part-time work. He was becoming more versed in social media, and then we started doing live sessions together.

Gradually, I found myself staying on during a live after Dan was done for the night. That is when my presence began to grow.

I would like us all to challenge outdated mindsets and embrace a new way of thinking. I've experienced firsthand how brutal the online world can be with one of my earlier videos. It brought in about seven million views in just 24 hours and I faced intense scrutiny. The video centered around a house saga and didn't come across well to everyone; of course, everyone misunderstood its intent. However, it did help me grow pretty rapidly.

I was initially overwhelmed by all the negative feedback and consumed with what everyone was saying. Dan was a great source of support, and he urged me to see it as a test of whether I would sink or swim in the social media world. Enduring the scrutiny was horrific, but it helped me to develop a thicker skin and, in the end, boosted my confidence.

It is quite frustrating to deal with ignorance and close-minded people. If I were truly doing something wrong, why would we take the risks to share publicly on social media? People often project their issues onto others instead of reflecting on themselves. Attacking someone else is usually easier than looking inwardly at yourself, and that is a major problem today with trolls (bullies).

I don't see myself in any competition with other influencers. I follow and respect many people in this space, and while some content might not resonate with me, I prefer to ignore or brush off what doesn't align with my approach. There are many people whose content interests me, is funny, or inspires me.

I see my social platform as a space where I can stand up for important causes. Every day on social media, we are presented with new challenges and issues to address within the room, and having a voice in this arena is so incredibly powerful. This outlet has allowed me to accomplish so much as I strive to defend others and empower them to stand up for themselves in ways they may not have considered before. I want my followers to understand that I'm just like them; I don't want anyone to feel that I'm above them.

When editing my videos, I keep it to a minimum, as excessive changes will quickly drive me crazy. Although I invested in various tools, especially in the beginning, I like to keep things straightforward and simple. In the future, it would be great to have an assistant to handle some of the administrative tasks of social media. I appreciate the people moderating for me during my live interactions. It's easy to miss something, so having them is very important. At this point, I manage many aspects of my platforms on my own. I have sometimes collaborated with Dan on specific projects. Still, lately, I've been working independently, aside from our specific go-live nights. This has allowed me to connect genuinely with my audience while keeping true to my vision.

You might wonder about the effects of social media and how it has impacted my family, particularly my children. Admittedly, constantly having cameras rolling can be a nuisance. Despite all that, my kids have witnessed many positive outcomes from the chronic exposure. Even if they don't always acknowledge it, they recognize the benefits of the visibility and the opportunities my online presence brings. It was a new rhythm to adjust to.

I make it a point to create a post every day, despite the challenges of fitting it into my schedule. Balancing family life with my social media responsibilities can be difficult, but I have managed to make it work. My contributions help support our household financially, and I find joy in fulfilling that role. In just the last fifteen years or so, the rise of social media has completely reshaped how families interact. I'm dedicated to growing my presence and establishing a meaningful legacy through my work.

Engaging with my audience gives me a different kind of purpose than I felt before. Dan and I are building together, something that is uniquely ours. We bring laughter and motivation to others, and while it can be exhausting, it's a fulfilling kind of tiredness. Social media has enriched my life in ways I hadn't anticipated, providing a sense of accomplishment and connection I deeply value.

Interestingly, we've built a global following, with both men and women connecting from all over the world. While Dan's audience seems predominantly female, I appeal to both women and men. So, I created the SAB brand. What do the acronyms stand for? It's about empowering both women and men, inspiring them to discover and embrace who they truly are on the inside.

One of the core messages of my brand is the importance of authenticity. When someone is genuine and transparent, it encourages others to stop hiding and admit their own struggles. Why are we so afraid to discuss our shortcomings? Life isn't always full of positivity, and not every day is filled with good things. My aim is to bring a dose of that reality into daily conversation.

My SAB brand stands for Strong Ass Bitch. It's an acronym that carries the weight of experience—every heavy moment we've had to lift ourselves out of. It remembers the sting of hurt, not to relive the pain, but to honor the healing. Because the sting fades, and in its place comes strength. SAB is more than just three letters; it's a movement, a mindset, and a mirror reflecting every part of who we are. It can mean Scared And Beautiful, Strong And Brave, Standing And Becoming, Sharp And Bright, or Strive And Breakthrough. It's Stand And Be (You), Smart And Bold, Still Always Becoming, or even Spicy And Blunt. SAB candidly captures the messy, crazy, beautiful, unexpected, magical journey of being a woman who's lived, loved, lost, and kept showing up.

Strong Ass Bitch isn't meant to offend—it's meant to remind. To push. To empower. To celebrate resilience. It's a bold declaration that we are here, we are whole, and we are not afraid to take up space exactly as we are.

It's natural for us as human beings to stumble and fall along the way; honestly, talking about our experiences is important. When we pinpoint and acknowledge where we struggle, it shows others that it's OK to face difficulties. We often become prisoners of our own fears and insecurities, but it's important to own our experiences and not be ashamed of what we've lived through.

Many people choose to hide their past, but sharing our stories can be incredibly liberating. Every trauma contains profound growth, and it's OK to acknowledge that we're not always OK.

I've hosted a get-together for some of my followers for three years in a row, starting in 2023. Each year, more people have joined in, and seeing everyone mingle so naturally has been incredibly special to me. I'm excited to continue organizing these events once or twice a year as a way to give back and show my appreciation for the daily support. My hope is that everyone who attends feels welcome, builds real connections, and has an amazing time. Balancing my personal commitments with the needs of my community matters deeply to me, because the connection we've built is real. The Zoomies are with me every day, along with so many other kind souls on YouTube and TikTok—and I'm so grateful for each and every one.

It's remarkable to see how far my journey has come in just a few short years. Initially when sitting by Dan during his live sessions I felt more like an observer than a participant. Fast forward to today, and I have a whole new daily routine. Each morning and seven days a week, I step on the treadmill and go LIVE as I engage with hundreds of people. This life change has been surreal. I have grown from someone who was hesitant to speak up, and now I get fired up as I connect with the people who share my passion for life. We have great chitchats—sharing stories as they watch me and engage with each other in the chat. I am reading all the comments there as best I can, and we keep the conversation flowing nicely. It makes the steps on the treadmill go by so fast.

You may wonder where I see myself five years from now. I would love a future filled with hope, health, happiness, and financial stability. It would be great to finish one book, and then I will strive to keep using my voice and share my experiences with a wider audience. What matters most to me is that you are all a part of this journey. Your support and encouragement mean the world to me, and I cherish the community we are building together. As we progress, I'm excited to see where the path takes us and grateful to have you by my side. We are creating a vibrant narrative together, and I can't wait to see what lies ahead.

Do you think that social media influenced your personal growth or perspectives? I ask this if you are also an influencer, spectator, or both. We are all engaging from one side of it or the other. Are you authentic in how you present yourself through the chat boxes or comment sections?

Since social media is such a big place and where a lot of the entertainment is these days, it can come with its own pressures of struggling to stay genuine. We all want to be liked, heard, and feel that we matter.

When we go live, people join us in real time. They don't just watch—they engage, connect, and become part of the experience. I love the moments where I'll see people chatting amongst themselves, asking how someone's Aunt Maggie is doing, how a test went, or if they're feeling better after a headache. It gives me such a good feeling to know we've built this kind, thoughtful little community together.

Of course, we get our negative folks who love to come into the room and break up the party. When all we are doing is maybe discussing buzz balls, the weather, pets, health stuff, or anything you can think of. We are doing no one any harm, just having fun conversations.

How do you handle negative interactions or feedback online? Do you brush them off? Reflect and try to learn from them if necessary? Do you find yourself defensive? Or maybe a little of all the things? It's hard right? I do hope that if you are a part of my community, you feel the camaraderie among us. I think I speak for all of us when I say that all are welcome, but we love to leave the negativity out. It's so cool that we can share real experiences from all around the world.

If you're new to learning about me, I welcome you to join in any morning during my livestream as I have my treadmill time. I try to be on consistently seven days a week unless something else is going on. We always love new SAB family.

19
A Snapshot Of A Day In The Life of 'Me'

A day in the life of someone else is never quite what you imagine it to be. You can't judge a house by its paint, just as you can't judge a person by the sneakers they wear. If we peeked through a window or snuck into a closet, you'd be amazed at what we really keep hidden. So, here's your peek at me. Yep, I'm an open book, and oh hey—you're reading it! Danielle

You may wonder what a day in my life looks like. Followers may see what looks to be one way, but the actual thing is not quite what one might picture. So, I will share a little glimpse of my life behind closed doors, offering an inside view of some realities I face each day beyond the camera. I rarely need to set an alarm because I have plenty of things that wake me up. I typically rely on my internal clock—or Ed. That is, unless one of my nuggets (what I call Josh and Rocky's kids) has a sporting event. In that case, I'll set an alarm "just in case." It would be rare for me to ever be in bed past 6:45 AM. On occasion, I get lucky with a 7:00 AM sleep-in on a Saturday or Sunday.

I begin by stepping my feet out onto the floor. The day starts early in the bathroom, removing my night guards. The animals are eager for attention, hungry, and need to go outside. After feeding the fur babies and taking vitamins, it's time to dive into chores, turn on the Zoomies, and get some videos figured out. Any remnants from the night before get cleaned up and often turned into kitchen chronicles content. A fresh cup of coffee pairs perfectly with tidying up anything Dan's left for me. Hehe.

Since my job is 24/7, work is already one of my day's priorities. If I'm not engaged at that moment, I'm always thinking about or contemplating ideas of what I'm gonna do next. Once settled, I can squeeze in a good 45 minutes of searching and brainstorming for content to post. All the while, my Zoomies are in the midst of it all. Then, it is time to explore the house and tackle some more chores, which often end with making the bed. I am always on the move. Sure, there are times when I don't feel like a lot of interaction, so I may spend a little less time with the Zoomies that morning.

Next comes my daily morning livestream, which I rarely miss. My followers know the routine and watch as I move on the treadmill for an hour or so. Then I wind down with my vibration plate and other equipment, with some stretching while we are still carrying on with our conversation. What I love the most about my treadmill time is that it's like an escape for me. It's the moment of my day when I can leave behind whatever mood I came in with, and I tend to end the segment with a smile on my face. I am able to release a lot of tension to shake off stress, and it's almost like I get to put on a little act. I'm not just running or walking on the treadmill. I'm also decompressing as I am engaged with the laughter on the livestream, moving from a feeling of blah and leaving with a lighter load.

It doesn't just come from the physical activity; it's a vibe that surrounds me. I get to see my regulars, share a laugh, and bond over conversations that help me forget about anything that could be weighing me down. I love that we can chat about almost anything in life, the world, and whatever might be going on. It's a great place to make connections and share moments without a lot of judgment.

After the morning treadmill workout, it's usually a quick dash to the bathroom. If hungry, lunch is next; if not, it's back to the day's tasks—maybe scrubbing toilets, tackling yard work, or cleaning up after the pets. The hours pass quickly, and before long, it's time to think about dinner, which usually signals showers—either mine or Ed's, depending on how the day is going. Some afternoons allow for a peaceful lunch break, often spent catching up with the Zoomies. On busier days, a quick store run might be squeezed in, and every now and then, I may treat myself to some Chipotle or one of my other favorite food spots.

I'm definitely the type of person who thrives on routine. I like knowing what's ahead, having a plan, and sticking to it. Change isn't really my thing, and I don't love it when something unexpected creeps into my day and messes with the flow. I prefer things to run smoothly. Sometimes, the sheer volume of emails, messages, responses, and phone calls can feel overwhelming. I don't like things piling up. Even something as simple as my DVR filling with shows I haven't watched yet gives me a little anxiety. It's not about the task itself; it's the feeling of falling behind that really gets to me. I like to stay on top of everything, organized and in control.

Throughout all of this, I navigate life with Ed, who is a constant presence. On average, Ed is relatively calm until lunchtime. He takes his time waking up, which is nice, so we don't have to rush. That allows for our mornings to be less hectic, more peaceful, and manageable. From lunchtime until bedtime, however, it's a different story. If he isn't wandering the house, he will drift in and out of his thoughts. This is what causes my routine to truly become constantly full of unpredictability.

Afternoons are for dinner prep, and once we've wrapped up a nice meal, it is time for our livestream or a subscriber live, depending on the day of the week. After a few nightly hours of engagement, I may reconvene with the Zoom friends for some casual chat. My evening tasks include laundry, or whatever needs attention I didn't get to that day. If possible, I like to be in bed by 10:00 PM, squeezing in some shows or a good book before I fall sleep. Since we installed a gate for Ed, it has made a slight positive difference. We no longer need to follow him through the house all night, allowing us all to rest better.

So, there you have it: a typical day in the life of Danielle Salinger. It may seem mundane and straightforward, but the reality is that navigating this daily routine can be consistently busy and often exhausting. Life can be overwhelming, especially when caring for someone with dementia, as circumstances can rapidly shift. Maintaining some balance is critical as it provides some structure amidst a lot of chaos.

When all is said and done, I'm still a human being. I admit that I have high standards for myself. While that can be a great motivator for me, it can also bring an unnecessary amount of stress that I don't need. There are going to be days I fall behind. Sometimes, things won't get done when I wish, but that's OK.

Because social media is what I do to bring in money, it is my career. Even though it can be tough at times, I show up. I know it's not just about me—it's about the impact I have on my audience, my family, and the future I'm building. Social media feels like a 24/7 gig. There's no clocking out, no real breaks, and it sometimes feels like a never-ending shift. But I'm hustling for more than just the work; I'm hustling because I want to be a big part of my family's success. I want to earn, learn, and ensure that I can help us survive and thrive no matter what's ahead.

At times, it's hard when the people around me, even my family—don't always understand the pressure I am up against. Social media influencers are easily misunderstood. People assume that it must be easy because we work from home or have a "flexible" schedule. So, what stress could I really have? But there's so much more to it. There's planning, creating, editing, and staying motivated in an environment where you feel responsible for so many people. There's this feeling that if I don't show up, I'm letting them down, which can put some guilt on me.

It is a balancing act sometimes. I have a group of loyal subscribers who pay for my content, and I'm committed to providing them with value. It is pretty infrequent, but there have been times when I need to say, "Nope, not today." And as much as I hate to do that, I've learned it's necessary for my well-being. Setting boundaries isn't easy, but I've had to embrace it. I'm a "first-take" kind of person. I don't have the time for endless retakes or overthinking every detail. I've learned that sometimes the "realness" of something unedited or imperfect is more valuable than it being all polished up. Dan and I won't do fake, and I've always wanted our gig to be the real deal.

Beyond the videos, lives, and posts, there's a behind-the-scenes world of planning, managing, and adapting to the ever-changing social media algorithms. I find it rewarding to help others and to help myself. Even when dealing with criticism, I've learned to set boundaries and maintain authenticity. I like to come up with ideas that are interesting or different. I aim to keep delivering content you can enjoy, engage with, and relate to. So, that's your peek behind the scenes of this content creator's life!

Maybe you are a content creator, or maybe you aren't, but where do we have similarities? You might work a 9-to-5 job or evenings. We all have expectations, deadlines, responsibilities, and pressures to meet. We all have to balance our personal lives with our work. So, how do you manage your work-life balance? What's the hardest part of your routine?

Maybe you don't have an 'Ed" that you're caring for, or perhaps you are helping with the care of someone close to you. You may be managing the schedules of little ones, getting them to practices, ensuring they are supplied with what they need, and keeping everything in order. Whatever your responsibilities are, we all juggle different roles that require attention, planning, and a lot of heart.

We can respect each other's roles, even if we don't do the exact same thing. In every scope of work—whether it's caregiving, at the office, parenting, in the hospital field, education, fast food, being a stay-at-home mom/wife, or the creation of online content—requires effort, dedication, and a unique set of challenges.

How do you think we can show appreciation for those who might not be in the same position in life as you and maybe don't understand what goes on behind the scenes? Some good ways I think we can do this are to show more care and try to understand the behind-the-scenes details. That way, we can gain appreciation and respect for a job we didn't understand before. We may listen to their challenges when we acknowledge how difficult someone else's task might be. It's then that we can offer support when needed, even if it's just listening, recognizing the difficulties and what makes it hard. It could sometimes be celebrating their successes and cheering others on. We are on a better path when we recognize that every role can contribute value, no matter how different from our own. It shows kindness and empathy. All of this goes a long way to show mutual respect.

20

Shifting Gears: Trading the Corporate 9-to-5 for Full-Time Mom-a-Care-Duty-Influencer

A fun and neat fact about my life is that on the Behar side we have quite a few artists. My Aunt and Uncle painted pieces that I still have in my bedroom. A lot of artistic family members! That is special and personal to me. Danielle

My career path began in the corporate world. I started in one direction, only to be led down a different path that brought me to where I am today. From a very young age, I dreamed of becoming a teacher. As we all know, life doesn't always unfold how we expect. We encounter many detours, closed doors, and unexpected opportunities. I could have stayed in the corporate world until retirement, but I became a stay-at-home mom, a role I embraced with honor. It was very fulfilling to me. As my children grew older, the timing was right for me to step into a new path as a social media influencer and caregiver for my father-in-law. With each twist, turn, and experience, this is where I've ended up today.

I graduated high school in 1992, eager to step into the world and make my mark. I began my journey at San Jose's West Valley College before transferring to Sacramento, where I attended Cosumnes River College. In 1996, I graduated from Sacramento State University with a Bachelor of Arts in Child Development. That same year, my husband Dan graduated from law school. With both of us newly graduated, the future felt wide open and full of possibilities.

During high school, I worked various jobs to help cover my expenses, including nannying and working at TCBY Yogurt to pay for things like gas. My first car was a generous hand-me-down from my sister-in-law Carrie's husband: a 1974 Toyota Corona with a stick shift and four doors. It was a true classic in every sense of the word. While I sincerely appreciated the gesture (and having my own wheels), it probably wasn't exactly my dream ride. I couldn't help but feel like I'd wandered into a deleted scene from *Pretty in Pink*—where the car steals the spotlight because heads were definitely turning! It had character—the kind that made dramatic creaks, clunks, and the loudest backfires, ensuring all eyes were on deck. Once I stopped driving it, Ed thought it was the perfect opportunity to claim the car as his own, so he started driving it. (Classic Ed, right? He'd never let anything go to waste if it still had life in it!) After that, my neighbor friend Kevin stepped in, and I rode to school with him. Then, in 1990, my mom bought me a Ford Festiva for $1,800, which felt like a huge step toward independence.

I have always enjoyed working with children, which led me to pursue a career in child development. I worked at a daycare center throughout college, where I discovered a deep passion for early childhood education. Even though teaching in a school had always been my dream, I never seemed to pass the teacher's exam. I was always just one point shy. While that was so frustrating, in hindsight life was gently nudging me in another direction.

While I was substituting at the daycare, a director position became available. I felt both ready and qualified for the position. The center served children from birth to school age, and I loved the dynamic environment that included infants, toddlers, pre-K, kindergarten, and after-school programs. What I appreciated most about the job was the flexibility it offered. I developed great friendships, especially with the assistant director, and the perk of bringing my kids to work while they were still young and not yet in elementary school was invaluable. This was especially a blessing when they were babies—being able to nurse and care for them while still fulfilling my responsibilities.

As my career in childcare continued to grow, I received a promotion within the company and was entrusted with the responsibility of opening a new daycare center in El Dorado Hills. However, over time, the excitement and energy at the company started to change. Expectations became more demanding and unrealistic. The new location was farther away, and I noticed more and more obstacles. Eventually, I returned to the original daycare center, stepping into an office management role. By that point, though, my priorities had changed.

Raising young children and running a household was a redefining experience for me, and it made me realize my heart wasn't in working full-time anymore. When my kids were still in school, I had to make the tough decision to leave the corporate world. It turned out to be one of the best choices I made for my family. While my career had helped me save a little in a 401(k) and taught me valuable skills like balancing and managing responsibilities, what I found most rewarding was being a present mom. It wasn't about working hard for a paycheck anymore; it was about being there for my children—attending doctor's appointments, parent-teacher conferences, and being involved in all of their activities.

I will always remember the years I spent at the daycare center. Working with kids was deeply fulfilling—helping them solve problems, watching their faces light up with new experiences, and celebrating their growth. It was such a rewarding time. Those moments not only deepened my understanding of child development but also gave me a front-row seat to the joy my own children found in their day-to-day experiences during those early years.

Dan and I faced our challenges, especially with managing medical expenses due to his self-employment, but we made it work. We saved where we could, made sacrifices, and worked together to ensure our family's well-being. Looking back, I wouldn't trade the opportunity to stay home with my kids for anything. Yes, it was exhausting at times, but being there for them every day—taking them to soccer practice, dentist appointments, and school events—was so fulfilling. I realized my life could still be meaningful, even without climbing the corporate ladder.

I had built a career that reflected my passions and values, and then I transitioned into being a full-time mom, dedicating all my heart and energy to the role that was most important. One of the greatest lessons I've learned through all of this is that success looks different for everyone. Fulfillment doesn't always come from a title or a corner office; it can be found in the small moments at home—like sitting at the breakfast table, reading a book, or nurturing the people we love.

Today, a subtle message often suggests that women are somehow "less than" if they choose to be stay-at-home moms. Many women feel pressured to pursue careers and titles. I recognize that not everyone has the option to stay home. While many women today work from home, others don't have that opportunity. It's not the same for them, as they still face external job expectations while managing home life responsibilities. Countless women are working hard in various professions—whether in daycare, nursing/health care, retail, office jobs, housekeeping, hospitality, food service, and many more. Regardless of your job title or profession, you need to see yourself as an incredible hardworking woman, contributing meaningfully in your own way.

When you look at your life, are you working the dream job you always wanted? It's a question many of us wrestle with at some point in our adult life. You may be right where you thought you would be, or life could have taken you down a different road than expected. What held you back if you were not where you thought you would be? Is it time, money, or the education piece that played a part in shaping the path for you? Could it be external factors or responsibilities that you didn't foresee that impacted the choices you made for your career? It's not hard to look and see where we feel we've fallen short of the dreams we had.

Is there something you can do or need to do to end up in a better or different circumstance that brings you closer to your dreams? Sometimes, we feel stuck or unsure of how to take the next step. Is fear holding you back? Is it too late to change directions? Does it feel too big to attain? I think these are natural questions that we all encounter at some point in our lives. Maybe you are in a situation where you would like to be a stay-at-home parent, but you feel like you can't, or doing so would mean significant financial sacrifices. In all honesty, life often comes down to what we're willing to give up or sacrifice to make room for what we really want.

I encourage you to take a strong look at your circumstances. If there's something you've been wanting to do or change, if it's feasible don't wait on it. Time is passing before our eyes, but there's always a way to start moving forward toward our dreams. It can begin with taking that first step. At the same time, finding happiness right where you are is also essential. Working toward a goal is always possible without losing sight of who you are.

Don't be too hard on yourself if you aren't where you want to be. Life has a way of turning out exactly as it's meant to, even if it's not what we imagined when we first set out into adulthood. We all have regrets, but they don't define who we are. I, too, could have regretted some of my decisions along the way. Instead of letting that regret or guilt get the best of me, I tried to use them as stepping stones to help me grow. Through all the many detours, challenges, and sacrifices, I see them as contributions to the person I've become. In the end, we don't always control the direction or the paths that appear as we travel down the road of life, but we can make the most of the journey and embrace the road where we end up.

21

Zoomies

The people who are in our lives every day may zoom in and out, but we've built a ZOOM community that stays put, and we've grown together within it. Danielle

Now, let's zoom through this! Throughout life, we have friendships that come and go. We'll have our people—some who are only meant to stay for a season, some forever, and others that we let go. Maybe there's a reason our paths cross. Sometimes, we're meant to play a role in their story, or they help to shape ours. As we go through the stages of life, our interactions with different people can change. Close relationships may drift away. Then, we suddenly recognize we've started seeing new faces showing up among us.

If you aren't sure what a Zoom room is, or never been a part of one, I'll give you a breakdown. Years ago, we had chat rooms on the internet, usually centered around shared interests or hobbies. With today's technological advancements, that idea evolved with live video. When I talk about our Zoom room, I'm referring to a private, ongoing space exclusive to the Salingers.

For Dan and me, social media has made a new way of connecting with people who would come to play a big part in our lives. We faced many imbalances when the world was living a new normal with the onset of the COVID-19 pandemic. I found myself searching for something more stable in the interactions of my not-so-social life. It became a whirlwind that I was trying to maneuver.

What began as subscriber lives on YouTube and TikTok, then came a suggestion for subscriber Zoom sessions. So, we went from just having basic subscriptions to the idea of hosting an ongoing Zoom meeting all day, every day. This allowed for a deeper, more distinct sense of unity among all of us and provided the potential for a revenue stream as well.

People can turn their video and audio on or off as they choose. It's like having a buddy system available around the clock, with flexible, low-pressure socializing. No need to dress up in your best attire—just come as you are! Pajamas, hair out of place, no makeup? Totally welcome here. It might not be everyone's thing, but for some of us, it's become a daily source of comfort and cozy Zoom commune-hood.

As with all new chapters in our lives, we can experience a lot of excitement in the beginning. As this was evolving, all of us were learning together. It was neat to see that through the opportunity to interact 24/7, our virtual family was available to form and keep in constant contact despite never meeting face to face. We were such a diverse group from various backgrounds and different locations. Our circle included people of other religions, races, and creeds, and we were united together through our screens.

While everything else in our country and across the whole globe was uncertain, the concept of Zoom was being launched worldwide. In a short time span it became the substitute for conference rooms in companies that replaced in-person meetings. People got clever and began using it to host baby showers, bridal showers, birthday parties—you name it—on Zoom. It turned into the new way to get together when getting on a plane or train to visit family wasn't possible.

It worked great for us but didn't come without its challenges. Within any virtual environment, we can learn fast that not everyone truthfully presents themselves. People can be charming and speak smoothly, but not everyone is the right fit for our exclusive, close-knit space. Just like anywhere, people want to belong—and we wanted to give everyone a fair chance. But it simply doesn't work when someone is deceptive or misleading.

Members initially volunteered and took on pretty big responsibilities but, over a period of time, did not maintain the commitment level they once had. This led to a lot of frustration and occasional disappointment which brought a lot of complications that we never had anticipated.

At one point, we were experiencing peak growth, but knew we had to make adjustments. We gradually decided to settle on a more manageable size to maintain consistency. The core group eventually stabilized at around 20 members, which allowed our Zoomie community to form a more cohesive network.

We only ever wanted our room to be where people could reveal who they were and not have to be fake. That was made very clear from the beginning, and there was a harmony we worked hard for. We thought we were building unity and a family while forgetting the distrust and discord elements that accompany relationships.

Despite the occasional hiccups, many strong bonds formed between us. We are there to celebrate the highs and lows and help each other through life's ups and downs. It may be in loss, personal challenges, surgeries or illnesses, painful days, and life-altering scary events like tornadoes. By the same token, we celebrate one another's victories and achievements.

The Zoomies had a collective experience when we went through the journey of a member battling cancer. Throughout her treatment and eventual decline, the group came together to offer her emotional and practical support. Having her there in our virtual space reminded us how the connection to other people can be very profound in our lives, even from a distance. We were able to rally around her, provide encouragement, and comfort her through one of the darkest times of her life.

When you can stay connected and always have a friend there, it's a nice invaluable feeling. Some members have even adapted and taken their participation on the go, which allows them to stay engaged even during their busier times. Not everyone has that option though, and we stay mindful of that.

Despite its perks, we have to be cautious of the downsides of a constant video presence. The continuous availability of support can trigger a dopamine boost, making it easy to become dependent on having someone there at all times—even if it's just for a smile.

Even without a shared community room, it's easy to overlook responsibilities. But we've developed a system of accountability, helping each other recognize when we've been online too long or possibly neglected important tasks. Whether it's the kitchen or other daily chores, we provide reminders and offer encouragement to stay on track, ensuring we don't overlook anything that needs attending to.

My relationships have extended beyond the Zoom room; I have had people visit and spend time with me personally. My visits reinforced the depth of our friendship and offered something in our lives in a way that is rarely seen. These people have witnessed the real Dan and Danielle, which has come to show how we are just ordinary people. They can attest to the fact that we are not being fake. I love that they see how genuine we are and that what I preach on social media is what I practice.

The Zoomies have played a significant role in helping me heal from losses I've experienced in other friendships. We've built our own little world. I've always wanted our safe space to be far from the toxicity of playground bullying experienced years ago. As adults, I encourage everyone to approach disagreements with respect. If and when a conflict should arise, I address those issues swiftly as soon as I'm aware of them. We don't allow any personal attacks. Discord only creates unnecessary tension. Attacking someone's character is harmful and undermines the supportive environment we've worked so hard to create. It's important to recognize and honor those who maintain respect.

The good things which have come from this arrangement have restored some of my faith in humanity again. While we are all on our own separate journeys, we are on a path that finds support and common ground. Our understanding and rapport within this group are unparalleled, and I am happy to say they are my backbone. Individuals within this circle have taken on various roles, even helping manage some of my social media. That extra support has been incredibly helpful in my life. We are all misfits that come with unique stories and struggles where we need help. Some of us are lonely, some are single, and others are married.

While many feel that there is nothing like the human touch, many of us in our shared room feel there is no substitute for the environment that's been cultivated through our day-to-day presence. We have gained true friendship, and love.

Have you ever made friends online that you've never met in person? It's amazing that in this digital age there's the ability to develop genuine bonds with people, ones that are difficult to put into words. Those on the outside may judge it or see it as weird. For some, the crew on Zoom has provided more support and time offered than even with close friends or family—the very people you'd expect that kind of bond from. This experience has opened our eyes and challenged the stereotypical idea of "blood versus water." Just like sometimes we feel more love and compassion from our pets, it's a similar thing.

Are there dangers in relationships with people you don't know personally? Absolutely. We've probably all heard stories—of people who've been emotionally hurt, scammed, or completely misled by placing their hope and trust in someone. Behind the screen there are often filtered versions of who someone might be—or even a completely false identity. Intentions aren't always clear either. Let's not forget though, that these very things happen offline as well.

Have you ever connected with someone and had others question it? Maybe they thought it was too fast, too much, or that you don't really know them. But isn't that the case in so many relationships—on or offline? We often assume we know people because we see them regularly, but that's not always the case.

These days, whether online or face to face, caution is necessary in all relationships. Sometimes we invest so deeply in someone—whether a friend, love interest, or companion—that we lose sight of our own needs and boundaries. The lines blur.

COVID-19 taught us a lot about human nature. When everyone was stripped down to screens and solitude, we saw unexpected friendships bloom—while longtime connections quietly fractured. People became outspoken. Some of the deepest wounds come from those closest to us.

So why am I saying all this?

Because if we dismiss every unconventional connection as "less than" or "not real," we close ourselves off to some of the most meaningful relationships life has to offer. The Zoom room gave us something real during an unreal time—a space to show up, to be heard, to grow, and to find the kind of friendship many people search a lifetime for. Just because it was born out of something unfamiliar doesn't make the love and loyalty any less certain. Through Zooming we've learned the meaning of being there for one another.

22
Hot Flashes & Hot Takes: Menopause Madness

You're Valid, You're Worthy, and Yes, You're Still Fabulous (Even When Sweating!)

> *There are certain life experiences we don't fully understand until we're in them. While we can offer support to one another, no two people walk the same exact path or experience it in the same way. Each journey is unique, even when shared. Danielle*

My menopause journey began around the age of 36, right after I stopped taking the pill. I sensed that something was wrong almost immediately. When my symptoms worsened, my anxiety only escalated. My body felt hotter than usual and more often. I experienced unpredictable mood swings. When the realization and confirmation from my doctor that I was starting perimenopause came to me, I was overwhelmed.

The physical symptoms have been daunting, with hot flashes, sweating, and itchiness all over the place. Sleep has been challenging, and I often struggle to fall or stay asleep. Some days, I lack motivation and energy. Though I have some normal moments, stress tends to make those moments quite brief.

At times it becomes hard to be able to look forward to upcoming events. If I'm completely honest, I've had to come up with ways that help me cope. I really have to prepare myself. Irrational thoughts can be persistent as my body adjusts to what's happening. Other symptoms, like hair thinning, decreased libido, and headaches, have been evident. Existing issues like my TMJ have worsened. It's been vital for me to maintain a regular exercise routine. Though I have stress, exercise helps to manage it, and balancing my lifestyle helps keep these symptoms more to a minimum.

I need to stay on top of things and recognize when I'm reaching a tipping point. The progression of menopause for me has been very challenging. I've experienced memory issues and irritability often, and it makes day-to-day life very difficult. However, I've come to accept that this journey will have both good and bad days.

If you're experiencing any symptoms, I encourage you to talk with your mother if you can. She has a lot of knowledge when it comes to her own menopause journey, and what you also might expect. Understanding how your experiences may be similar can provide very valuable insight. Although friends can be a great support, they don't share your genetics. For example, one might not understand that weight gain can affect you during menopause until it happens personally, so it could be easy to judge someone or say that they are using it as an excuse.

Your Mother's perspective can help prepare you. If you end up having that conversation - write down what you learn. Knowing what helped her manage her symptoms can give you a sense of preparedness. If you no longer have your mother with you, a grandmother or older sister may be able to offer some insight. Because I lost my mom at a young age, I now realize that having that discussion could have made things easier or helped me better understand what was to come.

Perimenopause typically begins in a woman's forties, but symptoms can start in your late thirties. Unfortunately, the earlier it starts, the longer the transitional phase can last. Periods can become irregular much earlier than we might expect. Plus, you must factor in the potential for hot flashes, night sweats, and difficulty sleeping. What happens when we don't get enough sleep? Well, mood swings and anxiety can become a thing for us, and they lead to irritability.

Maintaining a good relationship with your OBGYN is crucial, especially before menopause begins. Annual checkups can catch potential issues early, such as fibroids, cysts, or abnormal Pap smears. Addressing concerns early helps prevent more significant problems later. Routine screenings for breast and cervical cancer are also essential. If you have an OBGYN, it provides support and comfort, and being proactive about menopause can make the transition easier.

Though menopause can feel like an end, I see it as the beginning of a new chapter. I've fulfilled my reproductive purpose by having children and no longer feel attached to that aspect of my body. It's time to shift our perspective—there comes a time for the next generation to take their turn!

What we go through as women during menopause can affect our mental health. I heard somewhere that studies shown that a large number of women experience suicidal thoughts during this transition, which is a serious concern. Menopause can lead to depression and being aware of this can help us seek support before complications arise. Since I mentioned it, I do feel compelled to share the Suicide and Crisis Lifeline is 988. They are available 24/7 for anyone dealing with overwhelming emotions, mental health concerns, or just need someone to listen, help is available.

Hormonal changes affect mood and mental health, and the life transition itself can bring feelings of loss and despair. It's okay to reach out for help. There are many support groups online, and healthcare providers can offer resources you may have locally. Please don't ignore these feelings or assume they will go away. Take them seriously and talk to someone.

Menopause significantly impacts my daily life. Mood swings can happen suddenly, leaving me feeling out of control, conflicted, and angrier than I want to be. The hot flashes are overwhelming, and I can lose patience with many responsibilities. There are days when I feel overwhelmed and need to step away to collect my thoughts.

For a long time, I was on birth control to manage my symptoms. In some ways, it was supposed to give me a little more predictability and help make things feel more manageable. More recently, I switched to a Mirena IUD and an estrogen patch. It's still a work in progress, but I'm hopeful that it's getting me closer to managing the symptoms—at least until I reach the final stretch of dealing with all of this.

I look forward to the day when this journey ends and I can fully embrace a period-free life. Looking for the positives in menopause is a great way to help us cope. Before long there will be no more cramps, no more menstrual products to buy, and the freedom from planning around our cycles! We are at less risk for some of the reproductive issues we could endure. Hopefully our hormone levels will stabilize, and our mood and energy levels can reach highs not felt in years. So, think about that, seeing it as a new opportunity to have a more positive outlook on life? One less big hassle to deal with anymore once a month! If that isn't a reason to be optimistic - I don't know what is.

Exercise has been my grounding force throughout this journey. It's an essential part of my daily regimen. Making my bed in the morning sets the tone for the day. If my space is messy, it throws off my whole routine. Organizing my home also helps me feel grounded, especially when menopause throws a curve ball. Simple tasks like tidying up the dresser drawer can create a sense of accomplishment.

Family support is essential during menopause. While every woman's journey is different, having a solid support system can make all the difference. I encourage families to learn about menopause and how it affects us. Understanding what it entails helps to open valuable conversations. Families need to shift their mindset from seeing menopause as a loss of sanity to recognizing it as a natural life transition. This can create a nurturing environment and increase empathy for those going through it.

I've learned to own my emotions and be open with my household. If I'm in pain or irritable, I let them know: "I'm in a lot of pain today," or "I'm having a tough day with menopause." I may have to walk away from a situation. It's okay to admit that you need help and support. Sometimes, if I need rest, I don't hesitate to take it, even if it's not always feasible.

My husband Dan can be pretty funny about the whole thing. Being real, guys don't get it because they don't go through this, and they never will. He wants to help, but he has no idea how to show support. While he's not always the most supportive in the way I might need, we're learning together. Now I know all y'all girls with men are nodding along, right? Men, sons, even daughters—none of them really get it! Support groups, either local or online, can be a great help. You might also want to join a hobby group or gym to connect with others and feel engaged outside of your experience.

As much as I look forward to the day when menopause is behind me, though, I've heard hot flashes can persist into your sixties or even seventies. I'm holding onto hope that life post-menopause will be glorious. Right now, though, I'm sad, miserable, anxious, and irritable. The cramps are worse than ever, and it feels like nothing I've ever gone through before. I've never been one for NSAIDs; I'm more of a 'suffer through it' type. But menopause has pushed me to the point where I can't ignore it any longer—and might actually need an Advil!

Preparing my daughters for what's ahead has become even more important to me, especially after losing my mom at a young age. I'm determined to ensure my daughters have some type of understanding of this reality they will face someday. Just as puberty and periods are natural life transitions, so is menopause. We need to normalize talking about these things that tend to be something so many skirt around the idea of.

My daughters often say, "Write it down, Mom," and while we tend to put off these conversations, the truth is that we should share what we know. By talking about it, we can debunk misconceptions—like the idea that menopause only lasts a year or two. I've been experiencing it since my thirties and anticipate it will continue until I'm in my sixties or even later. It's essential to let others know that menopause affects so much more than just hot flashes; it impacts our minds, sleep, skin, libido, and, yes, even our hair. Understanding these impacts and preparing for them is critical.

We need to talk about it. Journaling can be a way to process feelings, and it can also be an asset for our kids. I'll benefit from this book as a resource, but not everyone has that. Many find it hard to open up about it, but we shouldn't. Why wouldn't we want to share what we're going through or learn from others on the same path?

Culturally, we keep so much private, but there's much to gain from being open. When we communicate candidly, we show it's okay to talk about the hard stuff. If someone asks, "Why do you talk about your women's issues online, or why am mentioning them here in this book?" I say, "Why not?" If you're not comfortable with it, that's okay—you can listen, read, and choose not to judge those of us who choose to share. In listening, you might learn something new that you didn't know before. On the other hand, if something bothers you, feel free to skip that part or stop listening, and move on with no hard feelings from any of the parties.

We owe it to ourselves and to each other to keep these conversations going. The more we are transparent, the more we can help each other. We're all navigating this journey together. There is some type of saying out there about how people perish for lack of knowledge, and that can be said when it comes to menopause. So much can be ruined in our lives and relationships when people don't understand that this is a natural happening that we experience as women.

So, when support is key throughout our journey, how do we begin to get it from those we love? It starts by letting them know that they are simply that – a key part of our success as we go through it. It's a nice and gentle way of putting a little responsibility on them to help.

How do we get the facts straight and tell others it's no laughing matter? I think sharing what the symptoms and impact of menopause are by way of books, videos, and articles is just the beginning of educating our support system. We shouldn't have to be defensive about something we can't control. When our families know that it's not just a physical change in our body but emotional, it will hopefully bring some empathy. The least we can do is give them some perspective and be open. If we clearly say "I'm dealing with a lot" and speak specifically to what we are experiencing with our bodies, we reduce the likelihood of them making light of the situation.

Is it OK for us to have boundaries? Sure thing! Set them and just do it. While we may at times laugh at ourselves, there is a limit. We need to express our need for more love and support instead of laughter or teasing from others. Try to let everyone know when you are having a good day and let them see you smile. It can be an experience you all face together and will only be helpful for everyone involved.

While we should never use menopause as an excuse to misbehave, we must also give ourselves the space to feel what we need to feel, if that makes sense. We can become defensive as a natural response to the need for peace of mind. It's important to do what makes you feel validated. It may seem weird, but sometimes, having a simple statement can make a world of difference. You could write it out and place it in different spots as a reminder. (Like on the refrigerator) An example of what I'm talking about could be, "Hey, it's me, and I'm trying my best. This menopause thing is getting to my emotions right now and draining my whole body. I wish I didn't have sleepless nights, mood swings, and hot flashes, but it's not something I can brush off or turn away from. You have no idea how grateful I would be for your support and understanding through this. It's hard to handle, but I do my best every day. Can you help me by approaching this together with me? I know you're not going to get it all, but as much as I'm trying, I would really appreciate it if you could try to accommodate me as well. I would love your support; what I need from you is real. Let's do this together." You could, of course, create your own statement and keep it simpler, but it's something you can use as a resource. Just be sure you express it in a way that shows that this menopause thing is serious, and you mean business in your determination to get through it successfully!!

23

A New Reality: Navigating the Unseen Pain of Fibromyalgia

Discovering Fibromyalgia

As if I didn't already have enough to deal with. What?? What is this now? Fibro what? Oh, come on! Just when I thought I had a handle on life, this new "fun" condition decides to join the party.
Danielle

OK, here we go. Now who would have thought of all people that I would be diagnosed with fibromyalgia? Honestly, I'm still processing it and that will continue for quite some time, I'm sure. Now that I have more of a clear understanding of what I'm coping with I can say that some days are easier than others. It can feel like a fight with my own body. For eight months the symptoms had been relentless, but I associated them with other things. The dull achy feeling like I'm coming down with the flu would come and go quite often. The pain could be constant, and some days it was so bad that I would have to sit down and stop what I was doing.

When you go through something like this, you begin to feel as though your own body is betraying you, which clearly makes no sense. More specifically I dealt with some headaches like migraines. I also already had my vertigo issue. It was hard to connect a lot of the dots. Along with this, there are the mental effects. It's a different type of anxiety, accompanied by panic attacks. They're very real, but I only connected them to the stress my body was undergoing.

By neglecting to acknowledge that something was happening in my body that I didn't understand, I was actually postponing the search for the answers I needed. My body was screaming out to me, and I ignored the warning signs. Maybe it was out of fear, denial, or perhaps I just didn't want to face the fact that there could be something wrong. I convinced myself that it was all okay, but I had no idea what was taking place with my body. I shouldn't have dismissed the discomfort I was feeling, but I was eager to keep pushing through. I was allowing some guilt to creep in with the thought of putting myself first being wrong. That guilt only allowed for more stress, which worsened the pain I was feeling. It was a form of self-sabotage by the way I prolonged facing the truth. I could no longer avoid it by making up excuses.

As I think about the road to my diagnosis it all began with my physical therapy sessions. I had been dealing with neck pain for quite some time. Knowing that I had stenosis, it seemed like a simple issue, only it was getting worse. As the pain seemed to increase, my physical therapist thought it might be more than just TMJ or stenosis, which I probably suspected as well but pushed to the back of my mind. So why was my neck in so much pain? Why did my head sometimes feel like it was going to explode?

My physical therapist referred me to a pain specialist. After the visit, an MRI was ordered. That's where we started to get more answers. Upon the appointment where we discussed my diagnosis the doctor mentioned to me that fibromyalgia was becoming more common, especially with women my age. It's not a black-and-white issue, so there's no clear-cut answer. Fibromyalgia is elusive. There's no single test for it. It's basically a collection of unusual symptoms that don't fit into any specific box.

It was very frustrating for me to deal with the discomfort and have no idea where it was coming from or why nothing seemed to help it go away. Living with unseen pain is something so many people struggle with. My brother Josh made a lot of sense when he explained how fibromyalgia is like when you know something is off in your body, but you can't put your finger on exactly what it is.

A harsh reality to life is that stress can be a major contributor that makes everything significantly worse. It can literally manifest itself through your body with pain, tighten muscles, and spirals like a vicious cycle. As I reflect on my own life experience, I'm coming to see the realization that perhaps the bigger stress events in my life, like my mom's death, could have played a big role that has contributed to me getting fibromyalgia. Now that is just one trigger among many, but that was probably the big one.

I want to bring this up because, though it might be uncomfortable, I believe it's important. I was dealing with a deep sense of helplessness. I know I wasn't feeling suicidal, but at the same time I was really struggling. The feelings were intense and kept piling up. It became overwhelming and felt like it was consuming me. Not only did it affect my emotions, but my entire body felt off. For the first time ever, I began to understand how someone could feel trapped by immense pain and believe it would never go away. This realization helped me see how overwhelming suffering can make someone feel utter hopelessness, with no escape.

We never want anyone to think that there's something we can't handle. And that is true even in the midst of pain and chronic illnesses, there we are pressing on. Though we may have great strength, it often works against us because it prevents those in our household and families to truly understand the struggle we may be facing. We need more transparency. If it's in a gentle way, they may respect us a little more if we are honest about our challenges and in turn, they could develop more of an apathetic compassion to what we are going through.

Being diagnosed with fibromyalgia is a new reality for me and my life. I now must navigate pain that I cannot control. It's something that requires persistent patience. I've started looking into different treatments like steroid injections, and cortisone shots. Some people do massages and have found acupuncture to be helpful. Some try home remedies or physical therapy. I will probably go through a course of trying many different things to see what works. The main goal is to keep the pain under control, although it's impossible to completely eliminate it.

Fibromyalgia is an ever-evolving condition, both for me and for anyone else living with it. Naturally there will be days when I feel down and frustrated, and you know what? That's ok. I will look forward to the moments that I can embrace a break from the pain in-between the bouts of it. No one has this life mastered and everything figured out, it's a journey we all keep moving forward on. Fibromyalgia is a condition too often misunderstood. I intend to share my journey as a way of coping through it but also provide some hope through it to others. Fibromyalgia is not something we should ignore or pretend doesn't exist. It's a real, often misunderstood condition, and it's time we talk about it more openly, with less stigma and more empathy. As women, we carry so much, and sometimes our bodies remind us, or even force us to slow down, take a breath, and care for ourselves. It's okay to make space for self-compassion and allow ourselves the gentleness of rest.

As difficult as it can be to face another diagnosis, I want to use this as an opportunity to help others who may be going through the same thing, or who might in the future. When people hear me talk about my experience, it could later trigger them to reflect on something they remember hearing me mention, like, 'Oh yeah, I remember when Danielle talked about this... could it be?'—especially if they encounter similar symptoms and start wondering what's wrong. This knowledge could encourage them to seek an earlier diagnosis, get checked out sooner rather than later, and receive more support in coping. I'd rather be wrong about my concerns than neglect the possibility and let it linger and worsen. It's always my hope and desire that by sharing my experiences, I might help others who are going through or will go through something similar.

What are you being faced with in your life right now that you hate and have no control over? Have you received a fibromyalgia diagnosis or something similar? When we deal with a health condition that puts limits on us it can reshape our path. It creates potential struggles that would challenge us in ways we never would have thought.

Have you experienced chronic pain, heavy emotional weight dealing with life changes, or just knowing something was off and you couldn't put your finger on it? We don't get to choose what health ailments we will have. The bottom line is that we hate the situation, but we are in control of how it's allowed to affect us. It's a challenge that we have to navigate like driving down a dark road with a flat tire. We build our own strength and resilience as we face things that we have no opportunity to change. Sometimes life is gonna be messy, sometimes we aren't going to have it all figured out, but we have to keep on going. We are worth it.

Do you feel like you've been confronted with a situation like you're out of control and can't find anything to hold on to that provides a sense of hope? Whenever we are dealing with a condition or disease that has no complete cure, the game changer is for us to stay steadfast and refuse to allow the situation to drive us off our path.

For the ones who are fortunate enough to not be dealing with something like fibromyalgia, you are still a vital piece of our support system. To have empathy, understanding, and encouragement from others struggling through any ailment, makes a world of difference.

24

From Steps on the Treadmill to Cash Talk & Bank Accounts

We never have to worry about the conversation getting boring! Heaven knows we can go from tacos on Tuesday to shoes at Costco in an instant. Before you know it, we're diving into fun, unintimidating talks about real-life finances. This SAB (Social Accountability Buddy) loves learning alongside you, and we're all in this together—sharing tips and laughs as we go! Danielle

While I will never claim to be a financial expert, I believe many discussions need to be had regarding our relationships with money. We have all heard that saying that speaks about money being the root of evil, and it can feel like an understatement when we look at the state of the world. Financial health and preparation are crucial aspects of our life. It's never too early or too late to start financial education for our children or even for some adults. Healthy financial habits can make life go so much smoother. If money management were a priority in the education system, we could see less chaos and stress surrounding finances in the lives of all people. That is why I want to include this topic in my book to get us all thinking more about it.

The wealthiest people can have financial struggles. Not everyone shares or talks about it. Even billionaires have filed for bankruptcy, which shows that financial challenges are a universal problem. In a marriage, both people should be responsible for financial well-being and success. It doesn't always work out that way, though. From my own experience, I can attest that my husband Dan and I have faced significant conflicts about our money, especially in our early years together. I often felt financial burdens fell heavily onto my shoulders more than anyone else.

Stress and finances can be very overwhelming. It seems the more we earn, the more we want to spend. For me, the thrill of the casino is appealing—fun loud atmosphere. At the same time, it can also lead to very dangerous habits. Gambling can quickly turn into an addiction, as the excitement of winning can compel us to desire that feeling repeatedly.

It is normal for everyone to be frustrated about their daily expenses, as it is a common sentiment. Getting caught up in wanting more and feeling like finances fall onto one person is easy. I know what comes in and what goes out, so I recognize the need for adjustments to create a more balanced financial situation.

Saving money is a challenge many face, yet it is a requisite for financial stability. If only we could all find ways to prioritize saving some money, even if it is ten dollars a week or one hundred dollars a month, it would be a gain. If you can't do that, even fifty cents a week is something, and it will add up before you know it. How many of us remember having piggy banks when we were little? The goal was likely to teach us the value of saving for a rainy day. Some of our parents may have even promised to take us to open a savings account once the piggy bank was full. Yet, more often than not, it was spent on candy at the store before we even turned eight. This shows that the idea of financial success and its importance should start early. After all, where else do we form our relationship with money? How do we become great savers? Better examples truly make a difference.

The idea of having money that we can't spend right away can feel like torture, but if we shift our mindset from a young age, that 'piggy bank' approach can be incredibly helpful as we grow into our teens and adult years. A piggy bank with guidelines isn't necessarily a restriction; it's a smart way to teach kids the concept of saving for a rainy day or building an emergency fund. Rather than seeing it as limiting, it's a valuable lesson in financial planning and long-term thinking. Having safeguards to protect our finances can ensure better preparation for what life might throw our way.

There is not a lot of teaching in school when it comes to financial education. Because of that, it places parents in a position where they need to begin having conversations early on. Or at least they should consider this. For too many, it becomes a family endeavor many choose not to ponder. Everyone in the household can learn about money management. It is critical to prepare the next generation, as the financial decisions we make today will impact them in the future. As we consider our offspring, would you agree that we should ask ourselves what knowledge and resources we are leaving behind? Will they thank us later for what we showed them? By keeping an open dialog about finances and teaching these essential skills, we can empower our loved ones to navigate their financial futures more confidently.

Some basic principles can guide us toward healthier financial habits. If you can't afford it, ask yourself whether you truly need it. The idea of living within your means should create a mindset that says, 'If I don't have the money, then I can't get it.' That doesn't mean you can't save enough to be able to afford it later on. Some expenses are necessary for our day-to-day living. We have to prioritize. Minimizing debt is essential, especially for big-ticket items like cars and houses. Although small expenses can quickly accumulate, they can lead to overwhelming debt and derail our financial stability.

The more we earn, the more we often spend before considering saving. This cycle raises an important question: Is anyone ever truly content? We tend to adjust our lifestyle to match our income but imagine the peace of mind that comes with simplicity and being satisfied with less.

It is easy to get into financial trouble when purchasing cars, houses, or other significant investments without fully understanding their implications. Having some sort of financial cushion to fall back on as a safety net is always a smart idea. It's essential to focus on building assets that grow in value over time, rather than accumulating liabilities that drain resources. I encourage you to avoid the need to borrow money whenever it is possible. Financial independence is actually more valuable than what money can buy.

If I were to experience significant wealth, I would feel a mix of excitement and responsibility. While being financially free is appealing, it is important to remember that luxuries are not everything. Many people like to blow money on things they don't need. The goal shouldn't be to have more material things but more in the bank for a rainy day. Regardless of how much we make, we can all get better at how we view our money, spend it, and save it. With the thrill of having a little more money, I might indulge in a few nice things. But my core value of money and things would not change. My main focus would stay on providing security and comfort for my loved ones rather than materialistic purchases.

Another thought on this is that jealousy is something that arises when other people perceive our success in finances. Have you ever noticed that people can respond negatively when we achieve something successfully with our wealth? It's incredibly disheartening, but unfortunately, it's a reality. People can find it hard to be happy for others when they possess something they want in a bad way. We should look deeper into our thoughts and consider what people might have had to do to own that lovely home, car, camper, patio furniture, etc. Not much comes easily for any of us, and we should be careful not to get mad, angry, or jealous. Instead, try to be happy for others; it might inspire the motivation to work harder for some of the things you hope to achieve.

If I had the means, I would probably contribute to some causes like Alzheimer's research. Still, first and foremost, I would ensure my children were secure and didn't have future financial burdens to bear. Raising kids is expensive, and many families do not truly grasp these financial demands until they face them. If you think about it when raising children, over half of the expenses go to the children's needs. It can sometimes extend beyond eighteen years of age, especially when considering college costs. Every family dynamic is different, but we should negotiate openly with our kids about the financial expectations to avoid placing any unexpected burdens on them later.

Many households end up in debt due to overspending or making unwise financial decisions. It's easy to lose track of our spending, especially if we are impulsive and seek to fulfill many temporary desires. Once we start earning money, we should consider the long-term implications of our financial decisions. When you think of teenagers who get their first job, they all handle the newness of having their own money differently. Some splurge, some save, some are very giving, and some don't want to share what they feel they work hard for. Many of the ways these kids handle their money reflects what they have seen in their homes growing up.

Having good financial awareness and spending habits is attainable. Being aware, planning appropriately, saying no to things we don't need, and waiting for a later time are just a few ways we can readjust. What are we obligating ourselves to that we do not need? Remember no one has mastered this. Everyone faces money challenges and has to learn through the process. Questions like, 'How will I pay this off?' and 'Can I truly afford this?' should guide our choices.

When we are more mindful of what we spend our money on, it can be just like putting the right food in our body - it contributes to better financial health. When you think about collecting items or shopping as a coping mechanism, it is just like drug and alcohol abuse. It's crucial to recognize when spending becomes excessive and ensure we're prepared for unexpected expenses later. Ultimately, we should take responsibility for our financial inheritance (before and after). For example, ensure you have some life insurance to plan for end-of-life expenses. We should always consider the stress on our loved ones that can come from neglecting these responsibilities. Aiming to avoid this takes the burden off others later on.

Our money mindset should remind us that wealth will never solve our problems. Even those who are very rich should still budget and hold themselves accountable. Financial health, like every other area of our lives, requires self-reflection and room to grow. I don't share this to preach but rather to express that in my own journey, I am working to improve my financial habits. I hope to share the lessons I learn along the way. Together, we can strive for better financial awareness and responsibility.

Money cannot buy love, friendship, or true happiness; to believe any differently would be delusional. My husband Dan often reflects on the happiest times in our relationship when we lived simply in the small apartment we had when we were first together. We were solely focused on each other and our dreams. Back then, we had very little, but we found joy in the simplicity of our life together.

As we accumulate wealth and possessions, we inevitably invite more complications and stress into our lives. The more we have - space, a larger home, or material belongings - the greater our responsibilities become. When it was just Dan and me enjoying a straightforward life, that simplicity actually brought us some contentment and peace of mind. I remember living on basics, like frozen French fries, and I was perfectly OK with that. Through time, though, we acquire more stuff. We invest in family pets and buy the kid's toys and electronics, phones, and things that need updating. We may not consider the cost of a basic purchase over time. Then we have to invest more money to maintain them.

While money can bring a sense of security to our lives and provide convenience, it doesn't guarantee that we will be wise in our decisions. It is important to reflect on the lessons we have learned over the years when it comes to our finances. What have you discovered about your relationship with money? How can you plan better for the future? Have you taken time to evaluate your financial habits? These are critical questions; normalizing a chaotic financial life doesn't benefit anyone.

If we can find someone in our lives that we trust, there is great value in having honest, open conversations about many aspects of money. When we converse with people who are on the same page, they can speak from their own experiences, mistakes, and successes. Even getting a financial adviser can help if it's within your means. We all have different preferences when it comes to financial decisions—some may choose renting instead of owning a home or leasing rather than buying a car. In the end, any financial decisions you make should align with your individual lifestyle and values. As we evaluate and navigate our financial journeys, we should prioritize what brings us real happiness.

I would love it if this chapter allowed you to think genuinely about ways to help with your finances. I wanted to bring thought and hopefully provoke some ideas for you and me to help us all improve our financial well-being. An old truth about personal finances is that they add up over time if we save a penny. When we empty out that soda bottle or box we once filled with loose change, you'll be amazed at how much you've saved up. While thinking about saving (even small amounts of money, loose change, or even that penny), it's also invaluable to consider where you can cut costs and rethink purchases. Where can you cut back without affecting your quality of life? It can be as easy as brewing some coffee at home instead of buying it on the go daily. Those few minutes save you time waiting in a long line at the drive-thru and a few dollars in your wallet. Make it a special treat once a week or every other day. Some like heading into the workplace with a coffeehouse cup in hand, while others enjoy choosing a fun mug to bring along. To each their own—but whatever you choose, make it practical.

I challenge us all to set some specific savings goals. It could be saving for an emergency fund, a vacation, or retirement preparations and having clear objectives that help motivate us to diligently save more money. We need to keep good track of it as well. Building a nest egg is a huge gift to ourselves. We are all worth it. So view it as a contribution into your future. In that case, you (and/or your family) are the essential investment. One more stress taken away is another chance to enjoy life more fully. While it is a journey requiring patience and discipline, the rewards are all worth the effort. So, together, let's explore ways to build a better financial future, one penny at a time. Oh wait...Is that a tin can or a piggy bank I hear clanking with some change?

25

Hair Today, Strands Gone Tomorrow: The Letting-Go Journey

There's no sense in trying to hold on to the strands or glue them back on your head, but when you're faced with hair loss, you wouldn't believe some of the thoughts that go through your hairline to your brain... "What is a weave again?" Or, "Can I pull off the 'I'm just really into hats' look?" It's like your brain goes into overdrive, trying to find any way to salvage what's left...going out of your mind strand by strand. Danielle

Hair loss is a harsh reality that many women experience, but it's something that isn't talked about nearly enough. For many of us, it starts early and is a huge deal. Trying to navigate the devastation and uncertainty of hair loss can feel like a real quandary. There are so many potential causes, and it's not always easy to pinpoint exactly why it's happening. Stress, hormones from pregnancy and postpartum, chemicals, or medications are just a few things that can potentially cause it. It can simply be so many things. When it comes down to it, hair loss can shake you to your core because it feels like you're losing a part of yourself.

I first noticed my hair thinning after having my daughter, Hannah. I was only nearly thirty years old at the time, and it's been a long journey ever since.

I didn't know what to do. I wasn't on birth control anymore, and I thought that might have something to do with it. I became hyper-focused on my hair, stressed, and deeply worried. Six years after Andrew's birth, I realized it wasn't going away, and I found myself even more frustrated. That's when I had a conversation with my doctor, and it was suggested that I might be going through perimenopause. It was recommended that I try birth control again, which I did, but it didn't seem to help with the hair loss. I started using minoxidil and have been remedying it ever since. Honestly, I don't know where I'd be in terms of my hair loss without it. I probably don't want to find out.

Regarding treatments, I spent over $1,000 trying various methods, vitamins, shampoos, and different products. It all feels like a relentless battle that you have no way of winning. So, how important is hair really? For us women, it's a huge deal. Consider the social pressure – it feels as if men don't face anything close to what we contend with. I've often envied them, thinking about how stress-free it must be for them not to worry about dealing with hair loss the way we do. If they experience any thinning or balding, they can simply shave their head without a second thought. Even if they do it out of insecurity, no one really questions it. For women, though, it's a whole different story. Hair is often seen as a symbol of beauty, femininity, and youth. We may not fully grasp the extent of how much judgment is placed on how thick, healthy, and shiny someone's hair looks. When we reach the point where hair loss becomes our reality, we don't just lose our hair; we feel like we're losing a part of our whole identity.

I can recall watching some girls on TikTok shave their heads a few years ago as an experiment. They did it to prove that they no longer felt the pressure to live up to society's standards of having beautiful hair. The experiment freed them from expectations of having "perfect" hair, and I saw that it was incredibly empowering for them.

From my own personal experience with hair loss, I can say it can make you feel incredibly insecure. When I see myself in pictures today, I often think I look 'gross.' You might think it's just hair and tell yourself to get over it, but it's not just about hair for those going through this. I remember moments during the COVID-19 pandemic when I seriously considered shaving my head to escape the constant stress from hair loss. I felt overwhelmed and noticed even more thinning, wondering if COVID-19 was contributing to it. In the end, though, I couldn't bring myself to do it. I had been so tied to my hair for so long.

Back in my younger years, there was a famous singer named Sinead O'Connor who became well-known in the '90s. It wasn't just for having a beautiful voice but, ironically, for shaving her head. Why would she do such a thing? I recall that she did it as a statement of defiance but also made her more independent. She wanted to reject any of the expectations placed on women. At the same time, you could look at other singers like Madonna or beautiful actresses like Julia Roberts and Michelle Pfeiffer. Though undeniably talented, their looks and amazing hair played a big part in their public personas. When Sinead shaved her head, she showed us that beauty is more than just what you look like on the outside. It represented freedom for her. I personally saw it as such a bold stance she took. I think it worked for her. She was such a great talent, known for her beautiful voice.

Of course, it didn't come without controversy and media attention. Still, she used it to emphasize that it made her feel empowered. She could take control of her own image, free from any expectations imposed by others. It allowed her to reject the industry's attempt to shape her into something she wasn't, and she was free to be herself. Clearly, her decision left a lasting mark, as I remember it as if it were yesterday.

You rarely hear the question, " Why are you losing your hair?" It is not our fault. Period. Hair loss is not something we have control over. What can we target to place blame? It could maybe be in poor life choices or unhealthy habits, I guess. I've had friends who would save strands of their hair as they lost it. It might sound strange, but I understand. When you're losing your hair, it feels like you're losing a part of yourself, something you want to hold onto—like it's slipping away. If I had done that, it would have just been to collect the hair and track how much I was losing. Nobody wants to acknowledge the problem, but you must find a way to cope. I think in our society, women are often not viewed as pretty if they don't have hair, and being bald is frequently associated with illness, like cancer, or other hardships, such as alopecia. It's already horrifying enough, but dealing with society's pressures on top of that is just not fair.

One factor in hair loss that often slips our minds is that it can be genetic. This is not just in men but in women, and it often runs in the family. There is a stigma that hair loss is primarily a male issue; women experience this just as much, if not more, only in silence. Hair loss can be inherited through maternal and paternal genes. It manifests in different ways, such as thinning hair, receding hairline, widening parts, bald patches, and other forms. I've known it to start as early as the twenties and thirties for some people I know. Some teenagers get a receding hairline, and that goes for both male and female as well. Regardless of the pattern, hair loss is a personal and deep issue. It can make someone feel very self-conscious and worry about how they will be perceived and their relationship or career. It adds a whole new level of anxiety or feeling inferior. Hair loss doesn't stop at the head; it can also impact the overall body image and lead to social withdrawal from certain events or activities. Even though it may not always be visible to others, when a woman knows that she is dealing with a form of hair loss, she may be reluctant to be seen in a condition that is consuming her.

You may question how hair loss could impact your relationships with others. While it shouldn't, it can sometimes cause insecurities in different relationships. Some people might feel jealous that others aren't going through the same thing. Personally, I would never begrudge someone who doesn't have to experience what I've gone through—or what I'm currently dealing with. In fact, I'll admit that, yes, I do envy them. People don't always realize how lucky they are to have a thick, full head of hair. It's a silent struggle many women face, and too often, we don't talk about it. That's why I'd love to create a space where women can come together to normalize the reality of hair loss. Men are welcome to join, too. The more we talk about it, the less stigmatized it will be. I brought it up during one of my live sessions, and it opened the door for a big conversation. I remember some women were so relieved, saying things like, "Oh, you too? My God, I got you."

When going through something like hair loss, we want to talk about it with someone. The problem is we're often afraid to bring it up. It might be embarrassing, or we don't know how to start the conversation. Maybe we're just mortified and don't want to face the reality of what's happening. But when we normalize it, we can discuss the feelings that go with it. We can talk about the things that help us get through the process. We can ask questions and see what's worked for others. I remember trying a weave once, but I hated the itchiness. Through my online discussions with others, we started talking about ways to stimulate the scalp. Many women shared their experiences with hair toppers, extensions, wigs, weaves, and other methods they used to cope with hair loss.

I think everyone would love to find a "cure-all" or an easy fix, a single treatment that works for everyone. But finding support is essential—something we may not have realized we needed. Of course, we need it because it reminds us that we're not alone. We can go through this journey together and support one another. I hope this will help create an open connection among the people in my circles so we can help each other feel less isolated in our struggles. This can only help to reduce the shame and embarrassment often associated with hair loss, replacing it with the strength of a supportive community. Everyone is welcome, and this space is open to all.

Are you experiencing hair loss? When did it start for you? Are you clueless and don't know where to begin? Or maybe you've been going through it for a while and found some things work and others don't. Are you open about your hair loss with others? It is time to start here. So, beyond a bit of a support group, what steps can we take emotionally or physically to provide hope to us and cope with this reality we are facing? I think we need to reclaim control over our appearance and find a way to embrace the journey and have acceptance. What does that look like for us?

I think in reminding any of us who are going through hair loss we are not alone - we are off to a great beginning. It's not impacting just a few, one hundred, or a few thousand people. It can affect millions of people throughout our entire world. It's sad to say that this is a part of the human experience. Sometimes, that simple fact alone can comfort someone who knows they aren't so alone in this big world. I know I mentioned Sinead O'Connor, but if you do a little research, many other celebrities and public figures have had to face the challenge of hair loss. It may be a physical thing, but it is a highly emotional and mental experience. We must find a way to boost our confidence. Like with many other debilitating things, we must stay on top of this because it is critical to navigate through.

Remember that we are not our appearance. When I say you are worthy and important, your feelings are valid; be kind to yourself ...I am reminding you that your value is not defined by your hair or looks. It's okay to be upset about what you're experiencing, but find a way to focus on the great things about yourself. Think about your smile, or maybe you have pretty eyes. Some of us have a great sense of style, which can provide a nice boost when you think of those characteristics. We have to find ways to take the focus off our hair and look at the other things that are great about us. It's all about perspective. We no longer have to hide. If it's on your journey - it's a part of your story. When we face the music about our hair loss, it is then that we will own it and feel empowered. We must be patient in the process.

Hair loss is just another thing that is not within our own control. But we can sport new styles and experiment with different hats, jewelry, or scarves. People will often be prone to look at a pretty necklace or bracelet or make a remark about your cool sandals. Colors on a scarf cause someone to be less fixated on their hair. The other thing that can be done is to get us to think about something beyond our physical components. What accomplishments have we made, or what qualities do we have? What things do we have in common? Children, pets, spouses, allergies, television shows, and other interests. The list is endless. When we start to realize that our life is not set back because of something like hair loss, it will only lead us to better self-awareness. This can only empower us to look at the traits we have within us, way beyond our hair.

26
Embracing Aging and Real Beauty

You can't escape it, but you can certainly make a mistake with it! As each birthday rolls by, the number gets higher, and the story isn't written in ink in a book, but on your face with a few 'lines.' You can pretend it's not happening or get ahead with some skincare. After all, facing reality with a dab of cream never hurt anyone! In fact, it might just keep those 'life stories' looking fresh a little longer—and with some humor, those lines will look more like laugh tracks! Danielle

Let's face it, aging is inevitable, but how we approach this reality makes all the difference. We live in a world where it seems that youth is often glorified. As I've gotten older, I've learned that beauty comes from within, it's not just about products we use or procedures that we undergo.

It was a few years ago when I started taking my skin care more seriously. I wasn't looking for any magical cream or miracle product that could turn back time, because to me there is none to be found. Of course, moisturizers may be able to improve our skin and keep it healthy, but there's not a cream or serum that is going to turn back our clock. It's something that I've accepted along with the fact that the more we try to fight the aging process, the more we may actually miss out on the fact that we can enjoy the process itself.

I have two daughters that are looking at me and watching how I handle it. I've always told my girls to be realistic about what beauty and youth is. We have to embrace every stage of life. If you want to experiment with creams, treatments, hair colors it's all fun and well. There's something that can be even more important though that comes with accepting our age and loving ourselves unconditionally through the stages of our life.

I did make some mistakes in my younger years when it came to taking care of my skin, like using baby oil for tanning. That was so bad for my skin and didn't allow me to protect it as well as I should have. At this point in my life, I've made peace with the changes. I've decided that I'm not going to dye my hair anymore, that's been a while. It was a little bit freeing honestly. I know not everybody feels the same about these topics, but I'm just telling you what I have found works for myself. If dyeing your hair or using products makes you feel good, then by all means do it. For my life it's more about letting go of unnecessary pressures. Wisdom can come with aging, and I've made a decision to embrace things naturally.

When you look at people and observe them in conversation it seems at times that people are spending an enormous amount of time fighting with aging. The more we fight it—whether by noticing wrinkles and considering plastic surgery to fix them—the less we embrace the unique beauty that comes with growing older. Hear me out, I'm not saying that it's wrong to make choices for your body to get a procedure if you feel good about it. I'm just saying that we should make sure our decisions come from a place of self-love, rather than insecurity that would accustom us to be conformed to society's expectations and desires for us.

Let's be honest here, males are probably not held to the same standards as females. I feel the pressure is more prevalent for women. The culture we live in tells us we need to stay youthful to be beautiful, but I'm not buying it anymore. I won't be held captive to the idea that youth is the only form of beauty. There are many women and men who have amazing features and embrace them naturally, and that's something to celebrate.

So many take things like moles, birth marks, freckles, and scars as imperfections. People want these things to be different or nonexistent. There is no need to hide our beauty marks that came free of charge at birth, and we shouldn't run away from them. It's my desire to normalize what is viewed as imperfections. I show up on social media, I come as myself - imperfections, wrinkles, gray hairs, and all.

I am far from perfect, and you won't find me trying to be. If I want to wear my hat backwards or go makeup free, that's my choice. We all can ask ourselves the question - why do we use things that make us feel less authentic? If a procedure or product doesn't feel right, then simply don't do it or use it. If you're doing something to fit in some sort of mold or expectation it may be time to reconsider and reassess. We have to own our choices.

I do understand that not everyone is ready to accept the changes that come with aging, but let me tell you - for me, it's liberating. When we come to terms with the changes we experience in our bodies, with our faces, with our hair, we recognize that it's all part of a story we have lived. We're not moving back with regrets, but we are going forward.

I highly encourage us to embrace the next phase of our lives. If you're in your thirties, forties, fifties, or beyond, don't view aging as something to fight. Quite honestly, getting older is a privilege that has been denied to many people. We should give thanks for every year we live. Every rainfall we have has a story behind it, and every gray hair reminds us of something that caused the glitter to shine. To age is not the end of our beauty era, it's just the beginning of a new chapter.

When it comes to aging, our genetics play a larger role than we may realize in how our bodies change over time. We inherit certain traits from our parents. Skin type, bone structure and being prone to certain health conditions are factors that influence our aging process. That goes for both mentally and physically. Some families have excellent genetics, and you'll notice a lot less wrinkles and changes. Some men start losing hair as early as their late teens and if you studied their family history their grandfathers may have been nearly bald by thirty-five. While in other families, you might see men with full heads of hair into their sixties. We pretty much have to live with the hand we're dealt with, but we should consider where we can manage it, if at all. Some of our results are influenced by the lifestyle we lead and not always genetics itself.

The best thing that you can do is take care of your skin, hair, teeth, and most importantly, your heart. We should always try to be rested as well. There's a part of you that has beauty with every age, and what makes you imperfect, like wrinkles and scars, makes you unique. Let's work on normalizing the aging process and learn to celebrate beauty in all its forms.

What stands out to you about the aging process? As you are thinking about aging, what aspects might you be finding the most noticeable or significant? What scares you about growing older?

Are there particular fears or uncertainties that come to mind when you think about the passage of time and aging? Does the reality of not getting younger make you uncomfortable?

How do you feel about the idea that time keeps moving forward and we aren't able to stop the aging process? Does it make you uneasy, or have you come to terms with it in some way?

The process of acceptance is hard, but we can all do something about it. It is actually possible to approach getting older with grace and confidence. Stop trying to be perfect. It's a great idea to make exercising a priority. Try to eat as well as you can and make self-care mandatory. Allow yourself to have self-compassion. When you celebrate the experiences that you've had that have brought wisdom you may find that you are dwelling less on physical changes. Embrace the fine lines that mark the areas for maturing, even the gray hairs.

Stay open to change instead of resisting it. Just like in our youth when we were becoming young men and women, we had an opportunity to grow into new experiences. We can also do the same in this part of our life as well. We had societal expectations centered around beauty and confidence in our teens, so is the pressure any different today? That should tell us that it's not worth it. There are new routines that we can try, and they might bring more joy into our life. Be engaged more with the people that you have good relationships with, especially any of your friends and family that are going through the aging process. You can lift one another up.

Although this one is hard, practicing gratitude can be essential with embracing aging because it allows us to focus on the things we do have instead of what once was. There are some things that no longer serve us and it's time to embrace the things that matter the most. To age doesn't take away your ability to enjoy a good life, it can only make it better and well lived. Adapting to the changes is critical too. Sometimes we do things out of loneliness or stress, but it's important to discover what brings us joy. For me, gardening, planting flowers, and nurturing plants is my way of finding peace. Others might enjoy visiting a new bookstore and/or diving into a good book. Whatever it is, finding those simple moments of sunshine, whether through hobbies, small pleasures, or just a change of scenery can add a sense of calm and happiness to our daily lives.

Aging is a shift, and by focusing on health, relationships, and gratitude, you can embrace this change with acceptance and a positive outlook. It's not just about getting older, it's a journey that brings new opportunities for growth, joy, and fulfillment. Embrace the process, celebrate where you are, and find peace in the present moment. Aging isn't a destination; it's a continual experience, where each stage offers something valuable.

27
Friendship: Through Thick and Thin, Laughter and Pain, Honey and Vinegar, Memories and Milestones

Fun Fact: The first concert that I ever went to was Howard Jones at Great America with my best friend Allison.

Friendship is a broad subject that touches every aspect of our lives. I've had my fair share of experiences when it comes to friendships. From my younger years, it began with Allison, one of my dearest and oldest friends. Our story began in elementary school in California, where we met and still remain in contact today. From the very beginning, Allison felt like family to me, and over time, I became just as close to her family as I was to her. Her home was like my second home, a place where I felt loved and welcomed. Her parents treated me like I belonged, and I was one of them, which only strengthened our connection.

Allison and I were quite different in some ways. While I was livelier and more outgoing, she was quieter and more reserved, someone who could be described as calm. Yet, it may have been those exact differences that made our friendship special. We balanced each other out in a way that made our relationship what it was. We became 'each other's people,' always knowing that no matter what, we had each other's backs.

When I look back, I can't really pinpoint just one special memory because there's so many. Every moment felt important, whether we were enduring and trying to navigate puberty, talking about boys, or figuring out tampons together. Allison was more athletic, the sporty one, while I tended to embrace other interests, but it never mattered. We were best friends. We did everything together—homework, sharing lunch, listening to music, etc. There was always an unspoken trust between us. I knew I could count on her, no matter what. Like any relationship, our friendship had its ups and downs, but we never stayed apart for long. Even when life took us in separate directions, we always found that we were there for one another.

A few years ago, I stayed with her for my high school reunion. It was a great time of reminiscing, and it reminded me of the beauty of our friendship. No matter how long we've been apart, we can pick up right where we left off. It's like time doesn't matter when we're together. That's the kind of friendship we have—one that stays timeless and real.

Allison is the friend I could always trust. She knows me better than almost anyone else. We grew up together, and even now, after all these years, I feel incredibly lucky to call her my friend. Our friendship is a testament to the idea that long-time bonds don't break, no matter the distance or time.

Another close friend was Shelly, whom I met one summer while I was in Nashville. It was a simple, spontaneous moment—when I saw her, she was playing outside on a swing. Without hesitation, I ran over to her. Then I asked her, "Do you want to be friends?" That was it—we had a friendship from that day forward. In Nashville, where no fences separated the yards, it was easy to spot her outside, and our bond grew with time.

I spent my summers in Tennessee, so we had the chance to share many adventures together during elementary and junior high school. When I was in High School, it changed a little bit. Shelly even met my dad and Babs, which made those summers even more memorable. I remember being this brave little girl, seeing an opportunity to make a friend, and just going for it. Shelly and

I connected over our love for stickers, Garbage Pail Kids, and Cabbage Patch Kids. We even created a little club, complete with a club binder, which I still have. Playing teacher and house was our thing; we always found ourselves on the same wavelength, sharing interests and laughter.

Shelly's family was very religious, and I always felt I had to be on my best behavior at her house. Her mother was a stay-at-home mom, and her dad drove the Greyhound bus while her brother, Joe—who we called Bubba—was always around. Shelly wasn't afraid to say exactly what was on her mind, and while her home life was fairly strict, I felt a sense of protectiveness toward her. She had a strong personality, but there was a softness to her that made me want to make sure she was okay. I always loved that I had a pen pal throughout the year when I wasn't in Tennessee, so we didn't miss much about one another!

Surely, we had our kid arguments—mostly over silly things like who got to play the teacher or the mom in our play—but those little spats never lasted long. We were both stubborn, but at the end of the day, the fun always outweighed any conflict we faced. Because Shelly lived close to my grandparents, it made it easy for us to spend countless hours together, and when I think of her, the word that comes to mind is "fun." We just had childhood fun—pure and simple.

Even though we've gone our separate ways over the years, we have stayed connected through social media. We still have many fond memories from our summers in Tennessee. The friendship started in our childhood and remains a connection I treasure to this day.

I've been fortunate to have had special friendships at different stages of my life, each providing their own sense of connection. Growing up, I always had someone to turn to—Allison in California and Shelly in Tennessee. They were my besties, my partners in adventure, even though we lived in different places. I always felt a sense of belonging with them, no matter where I was.

As I entered adulthood, my circle expanded. At around nineteen, I met my friend Melissa, who opened the door to a new chapter of friendship, the formation of our group, the "Five Pack." We were a wild bunch, and as the youngest—since most were closer to Dan's age or older—I was the baby of the group. There are countless memories we created together that became defining moments in our lives. Things that ranged from attending each other's weddings to partying on weekends. Our tight-knit group grew even closer as we navigated life's milestones together. The births of our children were among the most special—they grew up creating memories with each other and right alongside us.

Over the years, the five of us have experienced many highs and lows—changing jobs, moving to new places, and losing loved ones. We were there for each other through all the transitions that life brought. Weekends were spent socializing, heading off on trips to Tahoe, visiting wineries, or simply gathering for family outings. It was a time of closeness, sharing laughter, and mutual support.

As with many things, time brought changes. We all know how life can shift—priorities change, and with that, friendships often change, too. COVID-19 greatly impacted our group, as it did for so many people. Different viewpoints emerged, and while some of us were more concerned, others were more laid-back, leading to a kind of distancing that none of us had expected. I had my own worries, particularly with my son's health and everything going on with Ed.

In those moments, no one really stopped to figure out what was happening to us as a group. We simply drifted to some degree. Time and energy are precious, and I've had to reevaluate where I spend both. I'm not bitter or angry, it's just life. I think a lot of people can relate to this when it comes to their friendships. How often do we wonder if someone truly cares if they don't check in?

I'll admit that maybe I was in a bubble with all I had going on—struggling, needing things from people they didn't know of and couldn't see. We often wonder what is worth our effort when tired, and time may not always be on our side. We don't have get-togethers as much as we used to. It saddens me when I think about all our fun—how our kids grew up together, the trips we took as families, and the weekends spent entertaining.

I still keep in touch with the group today, but our interactions have changed. We've all grown in different directions. I've learned to spend my time more carefully, prioritizing happiness and quality in the moments I'm given. Friendships evolve, and though the Five Pack is no longer what it was, the memories we made together will always be something I cherish.

Another friend I'd like to mention is Stephanie, who came into my life because of our kids—her daughter Taylor and my daughter Jennifer played soccer together. As fellow soccer moms, we formed a special bond that I hold dear. I absolutely love Stephanie; her family feels like a second family to us. We've traveled together and enjoyed summer trips, creating lasting memories along the way. There's something uniquely binding about the soccer mom experience—if you know, you know; if you don't, it's hard to put into words.

Friendships have always been a key part of my life. I hope my kids, having seen my experiences with my friends, will carry that understanding with them as they build their relationships. Healthy friendships are something I talk about often. We all know conflicts will arise, and we'll have different interests or disagreements. Over time, flexibility fades, and those differences might widen. But at its core, what really is friendship? It's such a weird thing, and it means something different for everyone.

For me, friendship is rooted in mutual trust, genuine care for each other, and the willingness to truly show up for one another. I've learned that one-sided friendships can be incredibly draining and aren't sustainable. Both people have to put in the effort. No matter how far you are from someone, whether it's across town or across the world, friendship should remain friendship. There comes a point when you either keep investing in the relationship or you let it go.

The tricky part is we don't always see how one-sided something is until it's no longer there. It can be hard to accept that maybe you've been the one carrying it all along. And that's when you start asking: Who's really making the effort? Am I the only one keeping this friendship alive? It's not enough to have a history together. Like any relationship, friendships need work from all parties to stay strong.

Life changes, time gets shorter, and staying connected is no longer as easy. I've always made an effort for the people I care about, but now at times I wonder who's making the effort for me. Having a shared past is terrific, but that only takes you so far. We must decide if we will bridge the distance or let it go.

Friendships are about more than just memories; they require ongoing loyalty and mutual investments of our time.

Here are some reflections for all of us to think about regarding friendships:

Ask yourself, what kind of friend am I? Are there any friendships that need to be reevaluated, and why? Who are you to others? Are you dependable? Do you listen and show your support? We should never have to beg anyone for their time.

How well do you know your friends, and do they know who you really are? We all want reliable friends we can count on.

Do you offer fun in this crazy life (or are you fun to be around)? Reflect on what excitement you offer.

Do you have friendships where you can be you? It's critical to be open and honest and not have to defer our true thoughts and feelings.

As time goes on, some friendships might no longer align with our lifestyles or share our values. Ask yourself what qualities you value most in a friendship. Think about a friendship that's no longer as strong or perhaps no longer exists. What do you think might have caused the distance? Did the fading of the friendship open something within you that may have taught a deeper lesson (maybe about you or just a relationship in general)?

Let's think for a moment to reflect on these questions. When we consider the importance of reevaluating our friendships, we must remember that they are a significant part of our lives. They play a part in shaping our experiences, emotions, and how we grow personally. For the friendships that matter to us, we want them to produce something enriching into our life. Having a mutual understanding and honest connection is vital. When a friendship no longer serves a meaningful purpose to us, we disconnect. At that point, they can drain us and become unproductive while taking time away. When we reevaluate, we give ourselves a chance to ensure what the relationship is or isn't bringing.

We all can be a good friend. Still, it's about the choices we make and the level of participation we take in maintaining those friendships. Ultimately, nurturing the relationships that matter most to us is important. The friendship we have with ourselves plays a significant role in determining the kind of friend we will be to others. When we take the time to understand, care for, and respect ourselves, we are better equipped to show up fully in our relationships with others. Being self-aware and having compassion for ourselves will serve as a great foundation for healthy, and enduring friendships.

28

Hold That Thought... I Want To, But I'm Not Listening Anyway

Who's responsible for fixing the signal? Wait, plot twist! Lost in translation! Crash landing approaching. Is it gossip? Is it an overshare? Hurry, we're about to hit 'send.'

Welcome to the Communication chapter. We can do better than this honest title, right? Communication can be a messy subject. Considering that my life consists of communication in various forms at every moment of the day, I guess we need to go there. I can't write a book without having at least one chapter with a heightened focus on communication with other people. There is a right way and a wrong way to communicate. Whether it's with the people we see in person, in our homes, at the store, when they get our order wrong at the drive-thru or restaurant, or when they give me the wrong date on the phone and I show up for an appointment only to be told I will have to come back because my schedule was incorrect.

We are all a work in progress when it comes to communicating. When you get into technical communication, it can become a very one-sided perspective. People are either hidden and shielded or outspoken and transparent. They are either kind and thoughtful of others or toxic, mean, and like to bully. Back in the day, I can remember writing a note anonymously, but they could track back based on handwriting. People may have used a typewriter. Many hurtful things were left unsaid because it was too much effort. Today, we can hide behind laptops and cell phones, but we've become braver in saying things to people we don't even know.

I think about this almost daily and often wonder if people were let out of a cannon somewhere in outer space. What was their upbringing, their learning style, and what made them who they are today? We all know that conflict can arise if our communication is broken, which only leaves room for us to be misunderstood.

As often as I deal with trolls or disagreements with people I love, one thing remains consistent: I try to understand things from another perspective. We want people to listen to us, but do we engage when someone else talks? Do we read words in a text, email, or social media post and, as we're reading, think about something else in our response or what we're cooking for dinner? If you yell something across the room when you walk in the door, it may start an argument or be perceived as 'you're in a mood.' A different result happens when you come into the house after running an errand, approach somebody sitting on the couch or at the table and give them a chance to acknowledge that you are there. When eye contact is made, and they are not looking into another area or at their phone, it can make us feel like they might be considering what is being said.

How do we really know what someone is doing on the other end of the phone when talking to them? A good way would be to ask them: "You get what I'm saying? Know what I mean? What do you think about that?" When feedback is necessary, it also provides clarity that you're not wasting your time in the conversation. We may know what is retained based on the feedback given to us.

While it's not our concern if the woman at the bank is having a hard day, it is also important to remember that everyone has a story and a life they are walking through. We have to consider the mental wellness of many people we face on a day-to-day basis. This impacts communication and responses. If the dental receptionist just hung up on her husband after an argument and you're the next caller, it could show in her demeanor on the other end of the phone. Maybe the babysitter called in, or the guy handling the pumping at the full-service gas station is on his own today, managing the extra load. There are so many scenarios and while it doesn't excuse their behavior, it's something to consider.

Almost every job that anyone does, including social media influencers, is stressful in some way. If we are human, we can assume that someone everywhere is dealing with a type of challenge. Everyone is working on deadlines, keeping their house clean, balancing work and family, and anything imaginable that goes with the human experience. We don't have time to sit and talk and hear about everybody's problems, and that doesn't mean we don't care, but there's a way to say it. Would it be wrong to respond to someone who is being mean or hurtful by saying, "I assume that you're going through something, and that's why you're reacting this way?" Would that be mean? Would that be overstepping? Or would that show that we understand the reason for their behavior while also bringing attention to the fact that they may be a little out of line? Can we tell someone they're out of line without saying the words? Can we tell someone they're being nosy?

While we don't need to share every single thought that pops into our heads during a heated argument, there are some things we need to get off our chest. It's best to cool down and save some of it for a different time to see if it really matters. Sometimes, we critique people in a way that is over the top and excessive. Saying something like, "Since I'm being honest, I don't like the color of your hair and think you should change it back to what it was initially. And while I'm at it, your lipstick color is ridiculous," might be a bit much. Do people really need to hear all of that? Or do we feel dishonest if we don't say it? It's about knowing where to draw the line while keeping respect and honesty at the center.

How about when we pretend we don't hear something that has been said about us and people think we don't know. We're learning something that could later lead to a bad outcome. Sometimes, honest feedback, even at a time when it's uncomfortable, is necessary. And then you have the topic of insults, where you could say, "I'm just being honest with you," but how often are we honest with people?

Sometimes, we get people into our matters who shouldn't be involved; other times, we don't get people engaged in conversations they need to be in. Suppose there is a problem with a specific person—at the workplace, in the family, at an event, or at the store you go to every week to get your prescriptions—and an unresolved problem continues. In that case, all parties probably need to confront it. Maybe they don't know, perhaps they do know and think they're getting away with it, or maybe we'd handle things better if we addressed them more in real time.

Imagine if someone you know is on a pregnancy journey and shares their deep thoughts with you. Sometimes, we need to sit alone with what we are told and decipher who should know and who shouldn't. Before we share something very personal, like this type of matter, we should always ensure we okay it with the person first. Maybe Jimmy and Jenny wouldn't appreciate you sharing their fertility issues with others, even if your intentions are good and you know someone who's been through it. Of course it's good to make connections. But you can ask the other couple for advice without revealing who you're talking about. Include Jimmy and Jenny by explaining to them that you know this other couple or person who would be beneficial for them to talk with. They may appreciate it or could also ask you to refrain from that because they aren't comfortable. When we make connections, we need to do so in a way that respects people's privacy and ensures we don't overstep by checking if it's okay with them first.

Much of the world's communication issues today stem from saying too much too quickly, not saying enough fast enough, or simply sharing the wrong amount. When it comes to conversations, we need to know what we want to say before talking. It's not wild to aim for productive, healthy discussions. "Hurt people hurt people" is an expression many of us are familiar with. When it comes to unresolved pain or hurt, it can lead people to act out in ways that can affect others. When a person is hurting, they can become very defensive. It can cause people to lash out and even shut down—you have two extremes. You may find a hurt individual who is very hostile or sarcastic; on the other hand, they may be quiet and withdrawn. Either way, it can be tough to resolve conflicts.

We were all raised differently, and our forms of conversation could have come from many different backgrounds. We may have been personally attacked or criticized a lot, or we could have been praised to an unrealistic level. There are those of us who were somewhere in the middle. Constructive dialogue and addressing the unsaid things beneath the surface could be a way to create a healthier messaging style for everyone.

How do you feel you communicate? Have you really thought about it? If we're being honest, we all have room for improvement, no matter how old we are. It's something we can work on our whole life. However, if it can make a difference and cause the outcome of having less stress in our lives, it's more than worth it. The less we have weighing on us, the more unrestrained we are.

If you were to ask me for my top five keys to effective communication, here's what I'd say:

1) Be Honest – Always tell the truth. Do not lie. Honesty is like having a key and using it for the right door - without it you're locked out of having honest communication.

2) Listen up—Approach your conversation like it's 'on the clock,' not on a coffee break

3) Balance: Has anyone truly mastered the dip-to-chip ratio? Like, the exact amount of dip for the fifteen chips you grabbed out of the bag? It's a special technique I don't think anyone has mastered—not always easy, but totally achievable. Point being, share enough. But not too much

4) Empathy—Try to understand things from the other person's perspective. For example, wearing their shoes and suddenly being enlightened as to why they always have blisters! It's like them handing you their life's glasses, and when you put them on, you finally see things from their perspective. It's opening the door to more connection.

5) Feedback—Offering feedback ensures you've understood the message. This clarifies that you aren't on page fifty-six, and they are on page one hundred fifty-one!

29
Not Wrong, Just Different

What's popular isn't always the right fit for everyone; what works for some doesn't always work for all. The fit is different for each of us, the feel of it too. Keep in mind that every year brings something new into the spotlight, and what worked great for you in 1983 might still be exactly what you should be doing—or maybe the very thing you shouldn't. The real trick is finding what fits right for you. Danielle

Now, hear me out before you judge this title. We might think our way is the only way because it's to our own liking, or what we are used to. That doesn't mean the person sitting next to you is wrong for always doing it the only way they ever experienced! If you have never had blackberry ice cream, how do you know if you like it? Why haven't you had it? Why haven't you tried the additional forty-eight of the seventy flavors that are available at the ice cream store? You know what you like, and you know what fits. Sometimes, we are game to try new things. Most of the time people want to deal with familiar things. It doesn't make it wrong. Everyone has nonidentical habits and customs. If your parents didn't feed you ham and cabbage while you were growing up, that could be why you don't have much interest in it today. There are countless options for dinner each night. We all grew up with certain staple meals, and other families had things that didn't make sense. I remember trying stuff at my friend's house that my mom didn't make; some were good, and others weren't to my liking. Like when you go to a restaurant, you gravitate toward certain things on the menu you're familiar with.

We live in a world where society may trap us in a mindset that makes us believe that if we disagree with someone, the other person must be wrong. If only the idea could be embraced that we are all multifaceted people, each coming from unique backgrounds and experiences. Instead of placing labels on others, maybe start accepting that we are all emotional beings with many complexities. No two people have had the exact same experiences throughout their lives. Because we've led different lives, it's okay that they may not necessarily be wrong—just different.

There was a time in my life when I wasted a lot of energy holding on to things I had no control over. I had tense emotions and probably reacted without considering anything beyond my own thoughts. Could it be that I was just a human struggling to make sense of a world with so many differences? Looking back, I can say now that I wish I had been a little different because we often make life more complex for ourselves by misinterpreting others.

I'm grateful when I reflect back on how I have grown. On my journey, I've learned to take it a notch back and try to be more understanding about what others are thinking, saying, or doing. When I operate in this manner, people are more open to me. I have found that I now have a voice that actually empowers other people in their lives. My social media outlet has helped me express so many of my opinions and that pushes me to stand up for the causes I believe in. I feel gratitude for how far my life has come. I would go to the ends of the earth to fight for my children, to make the world a better place for them, my nephews, nieces, and future grandchildren. One way to do this is by encouraging people to think a little differently when it comes to how we interact with each other.

We all have beliefs in which we stand very firm, but many things are circumstantial. We often find ourselves pushing against forces that try to dictate how we're supposed to feel and live in society. The bottom line is that, in truth, no one can or should dictate how another person lives their life. There shouldn't be certain expectations for a man or a woman. So, why is this allowed?

Wouldn't it be better to tear down walls? Imagine if everyone began building bridges. If that is ever going to happen there needs to be a move toward having more meaningful conversations that don't result in disagreements. There's nothing wrong with respecting another person's opinion; in fact, it's the right thing to do. The world has become a damaged place filled with so much anger. People will often take a firm stance in what they believe in. Then they remain unopened to the idea that another person's perspective could be completely valid. It's human nature to resist admitting when we're wrong, and changing a mindset can be difficult. There will be room to grow when we realize that a big amount of the limitations we face in life are ones we've chosen ourselves, shaped by the perspectives we hold.

Take, for example, how divided the world has become in terms of politics. We often share similar beliefs, yet it's difficult to find common ground. We tend to focus on and build up the things that divide us instead of finding ways to nurture what could bring us together and expand. We would rather be right than take the time to understand where another person might be coming from. It's okay to have opposing views, and both can still have value. I've worked on it within myself, being more open to the fact that I don't have all the answers. I've learned that there's more to everyone's story than I can see from the outside.

For example, I strongly believe in women's rights. I believe that no one should have the right to control what a woman does with her body, how she works in her professional career, or try to change her identity in a way that weakens or diminishes her. No one else is living our lives for us. I'm not saying that I oppose anything about men; I'm simply acknowledging that a woman's experience should belong to her, guided by her own choices.

I've been very skeptical over the years about how I feel about the government and the systems we have in place to protect us. It could be because of so much corruption, anger, and selfishness. With this skepticism comes an understanding that nothing is ever quite as it seems. Let's begin to ask questions, stay alert, and always seek the truth—even when it isn't comfortable for us. In our times, truth is a hard word to come by. That doesn't mean a better tomorrow still isn't within our grasp.

When I reflect on the old days, as young as I can remember having recollection of, life felt much more straightforward, with so much that was uncomplicated. We had more unity. For example, when it came to wellness and health, there was no controversy about women working out to Jane Fonda VHS tapes, like I did with my mother in the living room. If it wasn't her, there was the fitness movement led by Richard Simmons, where we were all in the mode to look good. His videos were fun; they had people of all shapes and sizes moving their bodies for better health. Life was embraced differently back then. Maybe fewer and more practical options were the way to go. It was cool to be in shape, but it wasn't forced on anyone with a specific formula or the pressures we see today.

Over time, the glue that once held things together was lost. I don't know how much more divided our world can become; it seems hatred drowns out the possibility of conversing for unity. Everyone's quick to point fingers, looking for someone to blame for this, that, or the other. Where does that leave room for understanding? I don't have all the answers, but this is the state of our world today. Everyone faces struggles that don't have to separate us. If we could only be open and find a way to talk—by listening and being compassionate—wouldn't it be great if we could see a future where our differences didn't divide us but where the uniqueness in each person caused us to grow?

It won't happen overnight, but change can happen. Maybe stop seeing our differences as wrong and begin to view them as opportunities to learn; in doing so, growth will be found. It's not about being right, but about the ability and willingness to learn, grow, and realize that everyone is doing their best to make it in this world.

This world is shaped by diverse and unique backgrounds, and who we are as adults is influenced by life experiences. There has always been miscommunication between generations, and they struggle with differing viewpoints. I think the influence of social media has only deepened the divide within our culture. How could the idea that a person's individual experience or perspective isn't valid have been allowed? People are so quick to label others as wrong that they neglect how much this is causing further division.

When you look at cultural differences, you'll find that what is considered 'normal' can be quite divergent, and these differences influence how problems are approached. All of us don't all have the same priorities, which leads to contrasting ways of thinking and solving problems. There's an additional complication when you look at cognitive styles. There are those who may rely on their intuition or what they feel in their gut, while others think things through more objectively. If someone acts more impulsively by nature, it may be because they're guided by their emotions. This strategy is logical to them. Not everyone learns how to handle situations perfectly.

What if I asked where you personally think we suffer the most when dealing with the "not wrong, just different" perspective? Many would likely say it's a political issue. However, the hostility that exists goes far beyond that. There are many cultural tensions, instances of racism, and biases that persist in our world. The problem may not be others as much as it is in the way we think. By letting go of our differences, we gain the ability to celebrate the uniqueness of each person and use our appreciation of diversity to grow.

We need more of those cultural days where people share their favorite foods and traditions from their heritage. It's a beautiful way to celebrate the uncommon things. How interesting it would be to delve into where we all come from and learn more about one another. Many would love the opportunity to try new dishes and explore other respectful aspects of different cultures. It would be a wonderful learning experience to discover what makes each culture unique, rather than dismissing them.

Then when you look at the perspective of rich versus middle class versus poor, perhaps there's too much focus on money. Regardless of how privileged a person might be, everyone deserves proper healthcare, education, and to feel valued. Suppose we aim to be less misguided and become more thoughtful. Instead of limiting opportunities, imagine open pathways for people to advance. We might see the world's overall mental health improve if we embraced understanding instead of judgment.

So, how do we move forward? Can the idea be embraced that others are not the same as us? Can an optimistic person and a pessimist coexist in the same environment? A hopeful individual is focused on the potential for success. In contrast, a cynical person is more cautious and likely to address any risks. They both actually bring a lot of value, and here is where we can see that differing viewpoints aren't necessarily 'right' or 'wrong.'

Just as life is navigated using various forms of transportation, we each have our own preference for getting from one place to another. Some people have always taken the bus and may not understand or enjoy riding a boat. But how can they say that the other way is wrong if it's simply something they haven't experienced? It's in trying new things that we can learn what we do like or don't. Why not give it a chance? Once we try something new, we might discover that a train ride is a thing we love to do. Meanwhile, others who used to dislike the thought of flying on a plane found out it is their favorite way to travel!!

In the end, the destination is the same: we all want to reach an understanding, connection, and a place of mutual respect. It's not about how we get there but that we're willing to share the journey with open minds and hearts, embracing the varied ways people move through life. Ultimately, our shared destination is understanding one another and knowing that we are not 'wrong,' just different.

"It was so strangely awesome the first time I heard Danielle mention the 'not wrong, just different' concept one day on her morning livestream. It was something my Aunt June would often say whenever anyone started to disagree. She'd even sit down with us and try to reason through it, showing us how important this idea really was. I began to realize that so many things worked better or simply clicked when you embraced this mindset." Kristi Lyons

30

Unity Despite Politics

Politics is like a sharp, sticky, and unfamiliar creature among friends and family. No matter how you frame it, it never seems to align the same way in two minds. Consider carefully how you approach it and where you tread in order to preserve the relationships you have. Danielle

I never intended to put anything in my book dealing with politics. Still, when I'm looking at the current political atmosphere in our country, I think a few things need to be said. Navigating political discussions is so challenging. Dan and I prefer to stay out of the debates. Our thing is that we like to focus on what unites us rather than what divides us. We have seen firsthand how politics can break relationships. That's all the more reason why we need to have respect for others when our opinions differ.

I can honestly admit that I have voted on both spectrums at different times of my life for various reasons. For me, it's vital to vote in alignment with my values during those moments. We have to stay open-minded because not everyone will think or feel the same way we do. When having discussions, we need to listen, think before we speak, hold back what we might not want to say, and keep respect as key.

I worry more about our future than anything else. There's too much focus on party affiliations. Seeing how much division has come from politics and made our lives a battlefield is disheartening. It's torn apart families, friendships, and many communities. We have the right in our democracy to vote according to our beliefs. Still, when engaging, we must stay open and respectful to avoid poisonous arguments.

It is important to recognize that every candidate has their good points and flaws. We are all human beings. When we consider who we select to vote for, we have to look at the issues and qualities that matter most to us. This includes where they stand on health care, education, the economy, social justice, and environmental policies, to name a few. We have to research to see where each candidate aligns with our values and priorities, which helps us make a more informed decision. Another thing we can do is evaluate their track record, proposals, fairness, and ability to provide direction and insight into how they perform in the office.

I feel like we rely so heavily on social media and news outlets for vital information. There is so much misinformation out there. While there may be a few reliable sources, so much news leans toward one side or the other. We need more neutral news options. One way to alleviate some problems is to use critical thinking and fact-checking before believing whatever we hear or see. When we take the time to verify that information is credible, it allows us to ensure we are making more informed decisions based on accurate data. When we seek diverse viewpoints, we can enrich our understanding, and it helps us to steer through more effectively.

So why mention politics in a book about my life? A big focus of my book is exploring how we can do better. We have to own our actions and express ourselves without fear of what others think. Like it or not, politics can significantly impact our lives when it creates strain in our relationships and unnecessary stress. I always encourage you to have your mental and emotional health in mind. This means even regarding rhetoric and combativeness from others regarding politics.

We need to see what it is doing to us as people, as Americans, and ultimately affecting our whole world. I encourage you to always be kind and come to have conversations with respect. I'm all about having healthier interactions with everyone we encounter, whether at the grocery store, over the phone, or on social media. If we stay mindful and intentionally try to avoid unnecessary drama in our conversations, it will bring more opportunities for better connection, understanding, and unity among us.

If we consider ourselves first, above political parties, we are all Americans. So many of us come from diverse heritages across the globe, and there's a sense of pride in that. However, it seems that in our country, we tend to experience some of the most intense conflicts when it comes to politics, for motives that are hard to make any sense of. Let me ask you where you see yourself in your discussions with family and friends when it comes to politics. Do you find yourself defensive before the conversation even starts? Do you have any intention of genuinely listening to what someone is saying? Can we disagree with someone but still listen, even though our view will never change? We can still be kind.

So, where do we begin? I want you to vote. I spend many of my days telling you how you matter, and voting is an opportunity for you to advocate for issues that matter most to you. I want you to use your voice and allow your influence to direct your vote in your community and our country. It's an awesome feeling that we have a say and can support candidates who align with our values.

Diversity is a vital part of a healthy democracy. I would love to see us bridge the gap between the differing viewpoints and gain a kind, open, respectful dialog among people. By listening to each other, we seek to understand where our reasoning may be for our differences of opinion. Bridging gaps happens when we focus on common ground. People are often eager to impose their thoughts and opinions on everyone else, and that's the only way it goes with some of them. It may take a century to get our country back on track. So, it will take you and me to intentionally seek ways to make it better. We need our own initiative.

So, here's the thing. Suppose we want to achieve healing and unity among ourselves. In that case, we must start getting back to the things that focus on the commonalities of connection between us. When we reflect on how we all have family, relationships, jobs, pets, new births, habits, hobbies, and graduations, we can get our conversations in a new direction toward understanding one another again. If we create a more open dialog, it might be easier to start understanding one another. Instead of what we hate about politicians, what do we like about the people in our lives?

We can relate to others when we understand their personal stories. So, what life essentials do we have in common? We all need food, shelter, health, safety, and have concerns. We can celebrate our life events, acknowledge inevitable difficulties, and then we are able to create conversations that begin to take on more things where we are relatable.

A lack of knowledge, if you've never been through something, might cause you to not fully understand the full picture of a situation. If we've never encountered a particular challenge, we can easily overlook what shapes a person's viewpoint on a subject. As we gain knowledge and more insight into these experiences, we create a deeper understanding and empathy as we see the world differently. It still doesn't necessarily mean that that perspective is correct. However, it begins to acknowledge diversity in the background that causes people to have the beliefs they have.

Most of us have a common desire for community, the safety of ourselves and those we love, and a better future. When we focus on our shared values, one key value we all share is our children. They are watching the chaos unfold and how we communicate through it. They are aware of the arguments, hear what we say, and it impacts them. Don't they look up to us, seeking guidance in our actions and words? We have the opportunity to create a better vision for our future and reduce some of the division. It's time for us to come together as Americans and do what's right as we think about the future. What are we passing down to our children and grandchildren? Could we put our own agendas aside for the sake of possibly passing down less harm to the generations coming after us? Striving for unity should be non-negotiable and essential for the well-being of future generations. Let's give them a chance. What does that mean? It is a foundation for healthy relationships and a stronger, more cohesive society. If we want it, we have to reflect on the world we want to create and leave for them and take the steps to get there.

If we don't acknowledge this and take the chance to create a better tomorrow, and if something doesn't change there will just be more division and unresolved conflicts. Do we want future generations to face these same hindrances—or worse? Instead of making it harder for them, why not try to build a better society where they can thrive? We owe it to them, and their future, but we also owe it to ourselves.

Speaking of youngsters, I don't remember ever hearing such intense and uncommon perspectives during my youth when it came to political conversations. Our kids are impressionable like sponges, they absorb everything they witness. The stress, tension, raised voices, and heated arguments can leave them feeling anxious and unsure. I know it would have made me nervous if that had been going on around me.

That being said, we shouldn't completely avoid the topic of politics with our kids, grandkids, nieces, or nephews. They're already hearing things from television, social media, and all over the internet. It's probably a good idea to share an age-appropriate perspective, even when they're little. We guide them in so many areas of life, this should be no exception.

If we can create a calmer, more respectful atmosphere when discussing politics, it teaches them they can also communicate on these topics with thoughtfulness and understanding too. Sometimes, the best approach might be choosing when and with whom these conversations happen. That can be healthier for everyone involved. Children are going to learn about political systems and government history in school. When it comes to the emotionally charged climate we have today, I believe more of us need to be intentional in how we approach these topics with the younger ones in our lives. A little care now could go a long way in helping them grow into thoughtful, respectful adults.

Let me ask: What can we do specifically to cut down on some of the conflicts that arise around politics in our relationships? It all starts with our mindset and what we hope to accomplish. When we're on social media and come across a post we don't agree with, especially when it's political, we do have a few options. We can choose to do nothing and move past it, not giving it another thought. We can dwell on it and allow it to stress us out. Or we can comment on it. It's easy to comment on posts that we agree with and share our same opinions, but it's a whole different story when the content touches a nerve inside of us. When that happens, we may end up reacting in a way that doesn't lead to a positive outcome, which can fuel more division and conflict.

Some people set a strict "no politics" rule in certain social settings, and a lot of workplaces do the same, which can be a good thing. If you take a stance on political discussions, it can be helpful to politely let people know that you just don't discuss it with certain people or in certain circles. This approach can help avoid unnecessary hard feelings, especially when you know not everyone in the room shares the same viewpoint.

Now, there are times when current events make it impossible to avoid political discussions. Someone may bring it up, and it's important to be mindful in those moments. I try very hard to be sensitive and allow the conversation to flow while keeping it constructive. Sometimes, we can't help but feel hurt by what's happening in the world or our country, and I want to make sure that those around me feel safe to express their feelings, but in a constructive way that allows for understanding and respect.

I tend to avoid bringing these topics up myself and people know my stance on these issues, but I also understand that conversations like these are unavoidable at times. As much as we can point out the flaws in various politicians, it's more important to point the finger at ourselves and remember that our social media activity and responses are ultimately our choice. Whether we react with kindness or negativity is on us. Political drama is temporary, so why let issues create lasting turmoil we don't want? Besides, wouldn't we much rather discuss our trips, pets, ice cream sundaes, avocados, and great places to shop? Consider what we're flooding and suffocating the social airwaves with! Know when to delete, snooze, or block. Gain peace in this life!

31
No Two Happy Places Are Alike

Your happy place might not look the same as mine. It could be somewhere inside or outside, in a familiar spot, while exploring somewhere new, or maybe a mix of both. The bottom line is that our happy place shouldn't be too hard to find, it's where we feel that true sense of happiness deep within us. Danielle

I have covered many topics in my book, but this is another one that I couldn't leave out. Everyone wants to be happy, right? Happiness is a word that humans have the desire for. What happy means from one to the next is as unique as the individuals who are finding their way to happiness.

We've all heard about the "pursuit of happiness," but what does it really mean? Is happiness a place? Is it something noticed, or does it taste great? I don't believe happiness comes in the form of something like a box of chocolates, that fulfills everyone the same way. After all, even at the candy shop there are unending options! Personally, I would say happiness is a journey—a series of moments, choices, and realizations along the way. Essentially, it is something within us, and it isn't completely dependent on any specific factors.

Each of us has heard people say, "I will be happy when..." "I'll be happier when..." Bliss will come when I'm married, when I finally lose that weight, when I graduate, when I reach this or that success or milestone. But why wait for things to happen to be fulfilled? When it comes to joy, each person embodies things in a certain way, but true happiness is found in how we value our lives. It can be a little different every day. Happiness isn't attained by waiting for the perfect vision or version of our life.

Many observe others' lives on the outside, or pictures on the internet, and think they are living the good life. To some extent, the people we know tend to either show only the most wonderful happenings or just the bad things. It's two extremes. So much time is spent trying to present perfected images, yet they lose sight of the true meaning of what they're actually searching for.

When I look back at my own journey, I realize that happiness is often tied to contentment that comes from accepting life as it is. You can find peace where you are, even if everything isn't exactly as you'd like it to be. I think the times I personally feel happiest are those quiet ones—when I'm with my kids, surrounded by family, or doing something I love, even if it's small. The world tends to recognize happiness as something that comes from a big, bold emotional event. It can be as simple as savoring peace in the moment(s). For example, my time with my "Nuggets"—my nieces and nephews—brings me a deep sense of delight because I feel loved and appreciated. The little things—whether it's a phone call with a loved one, a walk outside in the fresh air, or watching a favorite movie—bring me contentment, and in those moments, I am happy. Even when the journey gets as complicated as it possibly can, there are still things to cling to that can bring a smile to our faces. Those are the joyful places found along the way.

Problems arise when looking for happiness in the wrong places. All of us may get distracted by things like social media likes, which is really just seeking validation from others. I might have a winning experience at the casino and think I'm satisfied, but it's short-lived. That's because it's temporary. So, where does that leave our happiness when all the excitement fades? It's okay to have these points in time, but we must step back to discover what really brings lasting fulfillment.

There's one thing that can easily get in the way of my happiness, and it's called my own inner critic. I often feel like I'm not measuring up to the expectations of others. Self-criticism is never good, because it robs the ability to fully be able to enjoy a moment of cheer. Focusing too much on what should be done or achieved can cause us to forget to celebrate the progress made or even the simple joy experienced. Happiness can be hard to find when fixating on what's missing, rather than appreciating what we already have.

So, how do we get there? It starts with becoming more self-aware. Take a minute to stop, pause, and reflect on why we aren't happy. If the questions aren't asked that cause us to dig deep within, we may never uncover the root of our unhappiness. Why be upset when others are experiencing happiness? Why are we really feeling that way? Could it be a form of judgement toward others or feeling threatened by their joy? Maybe it's a reflection related to something deeper that gets triggered, like jealousy, insecurity, or the fear of never experiencing happiness like they do. Not everything in anyone's world can possibly be great all the time. Although all of humanity probably does this, we need to wait before getting bent out of shape and start criticizing or judging someone who we believe does not deserve happiness.

There are probably thousands of books out there that talk about finding happiness. Even by seeking answers everywhere imaginable, no one is ever going to find a single recipe for happiness that fits every person the same. The media, including newspapers, the internet, social media platforms, our neighbors, our family, and friends all offer different ideas about what happiness should look like.

Have you ever noticed that some folks don't feel they deserve happiness if their life isn't complete? Or maybe because they've made mistakes? A lot of it can be social pressure, guilt, low self-esteem, and fear of judgment. Our society often refers to happiness as something that happens with a perfect life, flawless looks, and ideal living situations. This mindset may make people feel that they fall short, as though happiness must be earned instead of simply being embraced. No one should be made to feel that they don't deserve happiness. If someone is going through a hard time, whether financially or with their health, they may sense that they're supposed to act discontent—and that should never be the case.

No matter what's going on in our lives, we have the right to accept happiness every day. We don't have to make a reservation for when we'd like to feel happy; it can be there for us when we understand what it is. There are no standards to meet when we want the qualities of a happy day. If we wait for the ideal moment, or the perfect experience, it will never happen.

I often wonder how many individuals have never felt happiness because they truly don't know how to define what it is. Just as each of us has varying levels of pain, energy, or endurance, there are different perceptions of the thresholds for what makes us laugh, cry, or feel comforted. Experiences of contentment and joy are unique, and the same is true for happiness. It's a deep personal feeling, so it's not surprising that happiness doesn't look or feel the same for everyone.

Have you ever stopped and asked yourself, "When was the last time I can say I felt happy?" For one person, happiness might be found in winning a board game or indulging in a favorite hobby, like painting or listening to music. Others might find joy in the simple act of being with their pets or watching a comedian that makes them laugh. Traveling to new places can bring excitement and freedom for some, while others encounter satisfaction from learning something new or accomplishing a personal goal. It might even derive from gratitude, writing down what you're thankful for or taking care of your well-being by getting enough sleep.

We can't allow ourselves to forget that happiness can arise when helping others, because that is something which gives us a rewarding feeling. When helping someone put bags in their car and lift some of the load, their smile can bring the sense of a tug to our own heart. Sending a text to someone to tell them that you hope they are having a good day can make you feel good. Happiness, like beauty, is in the eye of the beholder. Discovering the things that resonate helps reveal what can be fulfilling in the moment, what brings meaning, and ultimately, the happiness we are talking about. By realizing that happiness doesn't come from being faultless or achieving every single goal, it's doing ourselves a favor.

By accepting ourselves for who we are and taking joy in the little things that make the days meaningful, life is lived differently. Did you know that when you judge yourself or others, it can bring unhappiness into the scenery? I think we often see happiness as a destination that can be reached, when it's found in the many moments along the journey. When realizing the need to love ourselves and become more self-aware, less is required to attain on a bigger scale. Many of us don't truly know ourselves because we don't see our value and appreciate the small things that bring joy. Now, I hope that this inspires us to more profoundly understand what happiness feels like and how to identify it in our own lives.

32

Forgiveness & Releasing The Hearts Burden

Forgiveness is like cleaning a dirty window. You see the mess, wipe it away, and regain a clear view through it. But once it's clean, let go of the cloth—don't keep it as a reminder of what you've just removed. Even if the mess was hard to clear, it doesn't change the fact that it can be wiped clean and renewed. You can move forward, carrying the lessons you've learned, but with a heart open to fresh perspectives. Kristi Lyons

A life-changing moment for me was when Dan had his heart attack. It caused a life shift for me, for us, and our family. We know things can happen, but it's in these moments we realize just how much we hold things dear to us. When everything transpired, the unpredictability made me remember how precious Dan was to me and how much I valued our life together. Who doesn't have their moments and flaws? But, when something like this happens, we reevaluate so much about our world. It was in those instances that I began to better understand how important conversation and releasing what hurts means, not just in our lives, but in the relationships that matter most to us.

When the life of someone we love is over we often live with regrets and say, 'I wish I had said or done this or that.' We may find a way to get what's in our heart out in the open, but too many times it just becomes a thought that we let evaporate and don't think much more of until the next time something tragic happens. Sad but it's the truth. You have to wonder why that's so.

Communication took on new importance in my life after learning the hard way through health incidents. First, with Dan, and then when my son Andrew faced serious health issues during the COVID-19 timeframe. Then there's Ed, whose challenges are further compounded by his dementia. There was no way to prepare for the day when his memory would start to fade. It could happen to anyone. That's why it's important to live the best we can and express our affection while someone is still able to understand. Even with Ed's condition, messaging remains key for us. It's crucial to show him tenderness in a way that he can still comprehend.

Ed's situation has significantly impacted the lives of all who love him, as it has changed the nature of the relationships we once had. We can still have heartfelt conversations, but it's not the same. The freedom of expression that once existed is no longer there. One thing that hasn't changed, though, is how much Ed loves and values his family. But dementia creates a new kind of forgetting that never truly disappears. It leaves us to navigate communication barriers, alongside a sadness that's hard to express.

Communication is more than just talking—it's the bridge between us, the way we connect, and how we understand each other's hearts. However, it's so easy to get things wrong. Misunderstandings creep in, and before we know it, we're misinterpreting the ones we love the most. We may even say things we regret that hurt, sometimes unintentionally.

We've all probably been guilty of sweeping things under the rug at times, pretending everything is fine when it's not. But that only keeps us stuck, with unresolved issues piling up out of sight. The things we ignore don't disappear, they build up, and eventually, they can become too overwhelming to handle. It's easy to ignore our problems, especially when life is chaotic. But that only leads to regret and unresolved issues.

The way we listen to someone is vital in what we will retain and understand about what someone has said to us. We need to be actively listening, where we truly hear what someone is saying. We can't be waiting for our turn to speak and think about what we're going to say when it's our turn. It's a skill that takes practice. I'm not perfect at it either—especially when life feels overwhelming and full of constant demands.

One thing I like to do with Dan is set aside time at the end of our day to share the highs and the lows. It's a simple question, but it opens the door for deeper conversation. It gives us the chance to express our feelings, share any frustrations, and talk about the things we're happy about from the day. Sometimes, I just want to be listened to without any response or advice, and I think it's important to be clear when we need to vent. Simply saying, "I need someone to hear me out," might be all we need to express. In the same way if we are looking for advice or feedback, we need to clarify that at the beginning of the conversation.

Communication and forgiveness go hand in hand, though they are not always easy, especially when we feel wounded by someone else. If we want to heal, reconciling is something we must actively seek. I've learned that to forgive doesn't always mean forgetting or excusing hurtful behavior—it's about releasing the weight of resentment. It's about freeing ourselves from the past, even if we can't erase the pain.

Dan once told me that I'd be thankful for the moments when I let go of anger and forgave without regret. And he was right. I may not always feel ready to let go, especially when it feels like someone doesn't deserve it. But it's as much for me as it is for the other person. It releases the burden to lighten the load I carry and allows me to move forward with peace.

Let's be clear: forgiveness doesn't mean everything will go back to the way it was. Sometimes, relationships never return to their original state, and that's OK. What matters is that we try to find a way to move forward—whether by letting go completely or setting new boundaries that allow for our healing.

Moving past it can be very challenging at times. When someone has hurt us repeatedly or a betrayal feels too deep to move past, those moments can be incredibly hard. I don't think we can ever forget the pain—it's not a simple fix. It doesn't always mean letting someone off the hook or wiping the slate clean. Often, it comes with scars that serve as reminders of what happened.

However, forgiveness offers a path to freedom. It's not healthy to carry anger and bitterness, and forgiveness is a way to release those heavy emotions.

There are times when the process of forgiveness involves acknowledging our own role in the situation. We may need to examine how we might have contributed to the problem, even if the other person's actions were more hurtful or wrong. We could still have played a part. There's no doubt that relationships are complicated, and we have to own our mistakes, even when it's difficult to admit where we went wrong.

When reconciling happens between two people, it doesn't mean you have to put yourself in harm's way again. There are situations where protecting yourself is necessary. This doesn't mean that forgiveness has failed, it simply means that setting boundaries is essential for your own well-being and emotional health.

Understanding the concepts behind a person's love language is often something people don't fully grasp. Dan and I, for example, have different ways of showing love. For me, emotional connection and acts of kindness mean the most. For him, it's touch. That difference can create gaps in our discussions. There are times when I don't feel ready for physical affection, and it's difficult for him to understand. But we've learned to communicate our needs, even if it's uncomfortable at times.

No one wants to feel taken for granted, and I think that in families, we can get so caught up in our own lives that we forget to check in with one another. In the society and times we live in, if you ask many families, you'll find they don't sit down for dinner together anymore. Everyone's schedules are full. We have to intentionally create moments of connection, whether it's a daily check-in or a weekly sit-down. It's vital for strengthening relationships and ensuring that there is no drift between us.

Ultimately, if we want to move forward, we have to consider forgiveness. But can we really let go? It won't erase the past or undo what took place. It's a choice to release the resentment that only weighs us down and keeps us apart. It frees us from the burdens that pain keeps holding onto.

We shouldn't allow the pain caused by one person to affect a future relationship with someone else. Sometimes, we get hurt by a neighbor, a coworker, a boss, or a close family member, and then hesitate to try again with someone who reminds us of that person. However, we should never punish someone else for the hurt caused by another. It's okay to be cautious and proceed carefully, but we must remember that each person is not the same and deserves to be seen for who they are, not for the mistakes of others. Life isn't easy, and the relationships we have can get messy. It allows us to reconnect with one another and move forward with grace while also allowing growth. As I travel my own journey, I remind myself that I'm not alone. We can stay disconnected, but in the end, we may miss out on something that truly matters.

There are times when giving a clean slate is simple, and other times when it's complicated and messy. We must find a place where we can learn how to move forward. I certainly don't have all the answers, but I do know this: when we choose to let go, we free ourselves from the past. Forgiveness is the beginning of creating space for healing and new connections.

Here are some deep questions to make us think: What is your love language? When you know what it is, it will help you to understand what you are looking for. How do you show love? Have there been moments when you've allowed silence or miscommunication to create a barrier between yourself and someone else? When you think about discussions, are you actively listening and waiting for your turn to talk? Do you think before you speak to avoid saying something you might regret?

Two of the most powerful tools we have to make any relationship work are communication and forgiveness, so why are they often the most difficult to navigate? It seems we often find it easy to misinterpret what someone is trying to say and then hold on to hurt feelings due to fear and vulnerability. Can you recall the last time you got everything off your chest, felt heard, and understood? Was it without judgment or assumptions? Think for a moment about a time when you might have held on to resentment or anger—how did that affect the relationship? What materialized for you as a result?

It takes courage to make amends and admit when we're wrong. Doesn't it take even more courage to confess something or ask for someone's forgiveness? When was the last time you told someone, you had a confession to make?

Perhaps they listened, and you found that a lot of freedom came from the weight you were holding. Could it be that reconciliation isn't so much for the other person, as much as it is for you? I think we would experience so much more peace of mind if we realized the depth of letting go. We may even forgive more often if we came to terms with the fact that unforgiveness holds us back from the true healing that could be waiting for us.

33

Trolls, Bullies, and What is a Ninny? Oh My! How We Handle It All with Humor Armor

The Trolls you encounter on social media are sort of like family—you don't pick them. They'll follow you, liking, hating, stirring and commenting on everything. But here's the twist: you get to decide how to deal with them. Block, delete, throw them out like old torn socks, or even have a little fun with them—after all, they're the unwelcome guests at your party. And you're the host!
Danielle

What do you do when you've built a community, only to be welcomed by the rage of a troll and bully community that doesn't seem to go away? Getting rid of a troll is like playing whack-a-mole—block one, and two more pop up with fake accounts ready to stir the pot again. So, my life builds up, I get reported on social media, and then I get silenced. The escalation can really take me down if I allow it to.

We know when the troublemakers are out on social media! Always. Every day. We may not always know their names (because they hide behind fake accounts), but you can be sure they're there to greet us with their daily attack. We may not have invited them, but they really should create their own club to terrorize one another! If you pay attention to them long enough, you'll get a full "How-Not-To Guide" on how to live life and treat others. It's emotionally draining.

The ugliness of people is almost unimaginable. They are trolls, bullies, and people who need a hobby. I have friends who almost have to stay away from following me because the amount of hate and harassment I deal with hurts them. It is a thief that robs one's joy and peace. We need an online version of No Bullies Allowed, but unfortunately, it's a part of life that we have to deal with. We have our task in the role of how to find a way to protect ourselves without letting them destroy when they come with their attack. As much as we wish it would disappear, it's something we can't completely eliminate.

The negative things in life help teach us how to cope, grow, and become stronger. There are benefits we can find in the negativity we're dealt with in life. Even the bad can help us in the end to develop into better humans. We may not see it at the time, but down the road, we'll realize how facing adversity, like dealing with problem people —helps us grow stronger. Tough as it is, there are lessons to be learned. Now, I know that men might handle things differently, but as women, we're already dealing with enough. The toxicity of others, especially when it comes from women toward another woman, is hard to fathom.

Here's where I remind myself: I am human. I am entitled to have my days where I have had enough. It just seems that on social media, we're not allowed that. We're expected to accept everyone's opinions, no matter what. But there's a difference between opinion and hate. What we're dealing with in a lot of cases anymore is a rising disrespect.

I probably doubt it, but maybe you are one of my naysayers and happened to pick up my book. I'm going to speak straightforwardly to you right now. Is your face red? I can almost see you twinge as you read that last line. Now, I hate to tell you this—and maybe you don't realize—but if I went to your house, I could pick you apart too. Is your laundry always done? Do you never get agitated with that one thing your husband refuses to fix? Or maybe you feel like everything is building up on you? Do your kids do all the grocery shopping, or do you live alone with no one to help? Maybe that's why you're frustrated with me, though I don't even know why you would be.

It seems like there must be something going on for you to spend so much time looking at my life, insulting me, and picking me apart. Maybe we should flip the script—how about you invite me to a live chat? Let's go on camera. Let's take turns picking each other apart. Sound good?

I am a strong woman who defends myself, and confident in who I am. I've worked hard to develop my sense of self, my boundaries, and my strength. I have overcome many things in my life, and it's caused me to build a life where I refuse to be trampled upon. I had to come to a point where I've built mechanisms to protect myself. I won't let anyone's negativity or criticism tear me down. But, in some way, that confidence seems to threaten you. Why does my strength bother you? Do you wish you could push back more? Is there a reason why you can't understand that, despite all the adversity life throws my way, I'm still standing tall and strong?

I say this with confidence, but truth be told, my strength is not a threat to anyone unless they feel insecure about their own place in this world. I'm not going to apologize for who I am or change something about myself to make you feel more comfortable. Maybe it's time for you to rise to the occasion and challenge yourself instead of continuing to be a troll. Have you ever stopped for just a minute to ask yourself if it really makes you feel better when you put other people down? Why are you always nudging somebody else with a negative statement?

Stop. Reflect on what you just said to me or someone else. Get in front of a mirror and say it to yourself—or send a text to you with the words you just sent me or commented on my post. How did it make you feel? Satisfied? Or empty?

I'm not saying this to hurt you. I'm saying it because I want you to take a long, hard look at yourself. In the long run, if we're being honest, the actions of being a bully won't make you a stronger person. They'll just magnify how pathetic you are being. Instead of continuing to tear others down, why not challenge yourself to build a more meaningful purpose? When you lift others up with kindness, you'll find power and strength that makes you feel like a better human being. You have to want it though, as much as I may want it for you, it's a choice only you can make.

Now that I may have caught a few trolls' attention, it brings me to my next paragraph...so hold on and stay with me. You won't want to miss this part.

Can you believe that people actually contact my husband about me? The bigger question is, why do they think they have the right to? Someone who's never met me in their life and wants to cause problems in my marriage... Let's think about that for a second. Is that maturity? Do they see my husband as playing more of a father figure role to me or something? Really? There are relentless people who love to meddle in our life, and I don't get it. Can you imagine that we just want people to know we're real human beings? We are a married couple that doesn't always agree with each other. Can you imagine that? I hate to break this news, but we've been married a long time, and we actually do support one another. When you're tearing me down, my husband Dan is also wondering why too. So, what's the purpose? What is there to gain?

Our family dynamic may be different from others. Our household might not look the same as yours. But if we looked inside all of our homes, we'd see that despite our differences, there are still many similarities in what it takes to be human, live life, and get through the day. So here Dan and I are, just living our lives, trying to be happy. Yes, we're on social media because people have connected to our story. They love Ed, but they love us too, and that's why our following has grown. But during it all, it feels like there are people desperate to be noticed, going to any lengths they can to burn my hide. Is that really necessary?

I went down a rabbit hole, looking through another influencer's content, just waiting to find something to pick apart, something to insult. But guess what? I couldn't find anything. Nothing to tear down. They had been talking about how they were dealing with trolling themselves. And here I am, intentionally looking for something to rip them apart for, thinking I should be a pro at it with all the harassment I deal with. But despite my best efforts, I couldn't find a single thing to be mean about. Funny how that works, huh? That shows us that this is a chosen behavior.

I'm proud of my growth through all of this. Do I win every single day? No. There are times I question myself. But in the end, I am me. Healing is part of my journey, and that continues until the day we die if we allow it to. Healing allows us to look at things as lessons. Maybe I'm a little confrontational, especially when people make demands while I'm sharing my journey. But we build stronger friendships without confrontation. I'm just plain and simple: Let's get it done.

Let me tell you, my friends, it's you, the ones who love me and the ones I love, that keep me going. You are the reason I keep showing up. People come and people go. Trouble makers come and go. They attack us, and then we see our committed followers, who we consider our friends defend us. And then the attackers start going after our friends. That's when we try to mediate, but we often wonder why it has to get to that point. We would love silence to make them walk away so we can have peace in the room. So we may block them, but they can't help themselves.

Will we ever put online hate to rest? As much as we want to...is there ever going to be an end to it? Where do we go from here? I'm sure there are books and tools out there that offer ways to potentially get rid of instigators, but I don't think there's an existing or defined path that works for everyone. I believe we need to limit our engagement because antagonists thrive on attention. In retrospect, that could also fuel the monster inside some of them. It's almost as if they refuse to be ignored. It would be great if responding in a more literal way, asking them specific questions to make them think—could impact their behavior. The question is, do they care? Or don't they?

We've dealt with agitators long enough to know: Be it in real life or online, they just want a reaction. When they see that their actions upset us, we're giving them exactly what they want. They continue to provoke because they get a rise out of us. When we stay calm and act like it doesn't bother us, they often get worse, digging deeper into their insults.

I've noticed that when a provocateur lunges in during a good conversation, if we don't respond, they may eventually lose interest. If they don't stop, we have no choice but to block them. We try to give them the benefit of the doubt. There are different types of bullies—some mean no harm. In fact, some even have helped boost our viewer ratings. If we dive into their life, we'd likely see them responding in a way that reciprocates the pain from being bullied themselves at some point. I think education is key, and sometimes it means leading by example and being the bigger person. Please don't confuse yourself into thinking that when I say troll I mean the cute bubbly fun ones you see on the movie screen. If you're a virtual pest, you're small—a small-minded person. Traditionally, trolls are mythical creatures, often ugly, hostile, and menacing. In the digital world if you're an instigator online, you're still just a small person, seeking to provoke and stir conflict for your own amusement.

Is there a way to really stop all the bullying in this world? We see it in our families, friendships, schools, politics, but especially online. It's everywhere. Critics do their best to offer us their bullying to belittle or abuse us. And this brings me to the word ninny—a word we've talked a lot about more these days. For those of us born in the seventies and eighties, we're familiar with it because our mothers used it a lot. It essentially means someone who's a little silly, foolish, or not the sharpest pencil in the box. I would say a ninny is like a harmless troll—someone who doesn't really mean to cause any aggravation. I'd take a ninny over a troll any day. But - don't be a ninny either! That could only lead to bigger problems with antagonism down the road.

I'm not a psychologist, and I'm not sure anyone has a one-size-fits-all solution for this lifelong problem. But what I do know is that I'd love to see change starting today. What starts small or seems insignificant has the power to create a widespread impact.

We need to make it clear that this is a troll-and-bully-free zone. And our reason is simple: we choose not to engage with those who want to hurt others. We're here to lift everyone we encounter. If it's possible to create a world where people help instead of hurting, heal instead of harm, then there you have it. Like it, love it, or don't—it's our mission, and we will not be moved.

34
Fit, Fierce, and Balanced: The Fitness & Wellness Duo

Danielle; Someone asked me if I thought that we need a new trend?
We don't need special skills to be healthy—it comes from within: your will and your desire.

We've talked about health and wellness, but fitness is another important piece of the puzzle. Although physical fitness is closely tied to health and wellness, it also encompasses more in terms of strength, abilities, and how effectively stress is managed. Physical fitness is not just about having a great body or looking good, it's also about feeling well, not just physically, but also mentally.

So, how is fitness really defined? I would say it's a mixture of endurance, performing activities to get moving, and body strengthening. One can contribute to fitness by taking walks, jogging or running, playing tennis, playing basketball at the park, running on the treadmill, lifting weights, following workout videos, going to the gym, dancing, and engaging in many other activities. Breaking a sweat is often part of a good routine. Fitness includes strengthening our muscles, increasing flexibility, and improving cardiovascular health. Getting fit helps keep our bodies working efficiently, provides enough energy, and can contribute to a long, healthy life.

Physical wellness is not about achieving just one thing. Like many other aspects of life, it is a journey that requires balance. We can all fall into that trap of thinking that conditioning is about mastering one thing perfectly—like drinking a set amount of water each day (with a quota). But fitness is more than just hydration or spending hours at the gym every week. It requires an approach that involves not only talking about your goals but also acting on them. How many people have bought an exercise bike or treadmill, only for it to become a storage rack for things piled on top? We have to make time to move those bodies, stay active, and remain committed to our well-being.

Fitness doesn't look the same for everyone, and that is completely normal. To be fair, it is about being in good physical and mental health, with enough energy to enjoy life. There are many ways available to us to enhance any wellness goals. It's alright to start small and then build up. The intensity of what you're able to do depends on your current stamina. Some people begin with light exercise and gradually work their way up to more vigorous activities that challenge them more. Swimming classes or walking in the neighborhood could be a great starting point. Remember that fitness is about improving and then sustaining those improvements over time. Start small and build up!

The approach will not look the same for everybody, but fitness and nutrition do go hand in hand. For me personally, I'm not a big breakfast person. I do enjoy a hearty lunch like a sandwich or an omelet. Others are very adamant about having a large breakfast, which is perfectly fine. The key is moderation. It's about making smart choices that work for your body. Also be careful not to get into extreme behaviors. Eating healthily all week and then binge eating on the weekends can become a very unhealthy habit.

Focusing on my physical condition keeps me grounded, focused, as well as motivated. Our inner critic has the capability to get in our way and make us feel like we're not measuring up to standards. A fitness journey is about progress, not being perfect. Whether one is using a treadmill, stretching, or just getting active, every movement and step counts. Even if the results can be slow to show, choosing to show up and try makes all the difference for personal fitness. Stress can be a massive barrier to physical condition. The more stressed I get, it becomes harder to maintain my stamina. A lack of sleep, worrying about daily tasks, and managing responsibilities, can take a toll on anybody.

We live in a world where judgment is everywhere, especially when it comes to body image. Society's view of health and happiness often revolves around meeting certain standards of beauty, size, and performance. These standards are unrealistic and do not define our true worth. Fitness should be about what makes us feel good, not about conforming to someone else's expectations. It's OK to embrace our bodies for what they are. We're not here to be the ideal version of someone else; we should focus on being the best version of ourselves. Bullying happens when we're not "skinny enough," or when we're too skinny or too fat. This judgment can lead to developing eating disorders and can change the course of our lives.

Part of my OCD stems from my anorexia, which began when I was 14. At that time, I starved myself. I wanted to fit into those jeans or thought I'd look good in certain clothes. There was also a desire for attention and to feel loved for my weight loss. I never really talked about it. I was afraid to share what was going on. Although I wasn't extremely skinny, it was noticeable enough. It was when I was getting sick frequently that things started to change. My doctor told me he was going to inform my mom about what was happening.

Because I have a history of anorexia, I all too well know the dangers and extremes that come with it. In the past, I pushed too hard with excessive exercise. My recovery meant that I had to find balance between exercise, rest, indulgence, and practicing discipline. Part of fitness is listening to and respecting the body's limits. Instead of obsessing about being perfect, maintain joy and contentment in the process. This is where a lot of people become mistaken because they think they need to reach a certain level, and then they're good to go.

If you haven't been in a steady fitness routine, it can be very hard to change out of the familiar pattern. It is very common to set unrealistic goals. This is where you will find a lot of people not caring about it until after the holidays, and then it becomes an intention they set for the new year. I've never been one for New Year's resolutions because they rarely last more than a month or two. True change can happen when we really think about it and set realistic, sustainable goals. Then we should individually commit to whatever system will get us to our progress. Being kind to ourselves and knowing that even the smallest effort matters is vital. We just have to keep mindful that we will not be perfect. Don't start January 1st, start today. Dare to be different about your approach, and not like everybody else who is failing miserably because their perspective is wrong.

Fitness isn't just about this month or this year. It is part of your lifelong path journey. Everyone ought to find out what works for them, balancing and staying consistent. I remember when I was young and doing the SlimFast method. I had two shakes, one for breakfast, one for lunch, and then I would eat dinner. Sure, it worked, and I was able to sustain my energy, but it was a temporary fix that would never have lasted my whole life long. Changing our mindset is needed so that we don't aim for temporary fixes, but rather lifelong wellness. To be the best version of oneself, living a life that allows for thriving is key. It's attainable for those who truly want it.

Let me ask this question: Why is fitness so hard? Is it motivation and drive? Could it be too many failed attempts? How has your wellness journey worked for you? What worked and what didn't? Some people depend on a partner or a buddy system, but issues can arise if change their mind, potentially causing your progress to crumble.

Does time restraints affect people? Schedule limits might be in the way of their family, job, and other obligations. Maybe some feel if they make health such a priority, they are neglecting other things. Be real about it. Maybe an hour, three or four days a week isn't feasible, but you can get up earlier and do ten or fifteen minutes of something or stop for a walk at the mall on the drive home. Sometimes it changes when people have gone through some sort of life trauma—health wise, relationships, job, etc. That is where consistency can be a factor in continued success regardless of life's circumstances.

Do some people give up when they realize it isn't instant? Or that it doesn't stay? If someone goes on a meal plan diet for six months and finds success, the second they change it up or stop, it will go back to what? This is where being knowledgeable and having proper guidance can make all the difference. Exploring options can start right in the kitchen or at the dining room table. Learn about what is healthy then add a little bit of items one at a time. You may find a love for bananas or avocados and can incorporate them more right into family meals. Change the menu along the way as well. Some people have force-fed themselves packaged stuff and they hate their way through a ten-pound loss that only causes more weight gain afterward. Don't do that to yourself.

Can somebody with physical ailments or limitations get fit? Absolutely! The problem is society tells them that it's out of reach. There are plenty of options for those with certain physical conditions, even arthritis or heart issues. If exercising is painful or difficult, a doctor is always able to provide some guidance. There are also a million ideas to be found on the internet.

Does support from others motivate you? I think it only lasts so long honestly. When someone sees a person is trying to lose weight, they may be encouraging in the beginning, but there are many factors why their support fades. It could be as simple as jealousy, or they don't have the motivation or sustainability you are showing. Ultimately, we are the greatest advocate for owning fitness goals!

We also can't allow environmental factors or resources to become excuses. Maybe there's no gym within five miles or affording an extra thirty-five dollars a month isn't in the budget. But what can be done? Stop focusing on what's holding you back and consider new possibilities about the resources available.

Many people focus on what they lack, instead of grabbing some dumbbells and moving their arms. Get away from those excuses and get that body moving. Truth is, it's much more rewarding to try than to make up reasons for why it won't work. If the environment is what's keeping that workout from happening, it doesn't have to be a roadblock. There are creative ways to get moving no matter what the situation is. No park nearby? No problem. Start by walking around the house, in the hallway, or up and down stairs. If you drive to the store, try parking further away to give yourself a bit more walking distance. Or, while shopping, take an opportunity to walk around a bit longer and browse, just for extra steps.

Watching TV? What an opportune time to stand up, stretch, or get moving during commercial breaks! Turn on your favorite upbeat music and just boogie!

While dancing, then slow it down to a walk or jog in place. Lack of space? No worries. Use a chair for balance and do simple arm and leg exercises right where you are.

Expensive equipment isn't needed to get in shape. Many stores offer items that can be just as effective. Retailers like Five Below and TJ Maxx have excellent starter equipment at a reasonable price. Start with a few basic tools, adding one at a time—perhaps a dumbbell this week, a resistance band next month—and gradually build up a routine. If money is tight, use everyday items. A couple of water bottles or a pair of old socks can easily become homemade weights when adding some rice or beans. There are also countless at-home workouts available online, ranging from push-ups and arm exercises to full-body routines.

The key is to set small, realistic goals and celebrate any progress. Physical endurance is about consistency, and maintaining a steady effort is as important as reaching bigger milestones. Think of your routine as something non-negotiable, something that becomes a lifestyle. By thinking outside the box of excuses, one can be amazed how many opportunities open up! Mindset can be a determining factor between success and failure. When approaching it with a positive, determined attitude, you'll find ways to work through obstacles. Fitness is about adapting, making the most of what you have, and staying committed. So, keep moving, one step at a time.

35
Kindness In Action: A Daily Choice

An act of kindness is almost a no-brainer. It shouldn't be that hard to be kind, right? Why would anyone intentionally want to be mean? I mean, really? I guess those people do exist, but it's not the world I want to live in. My advice to you is simple: pay it forward. Buy someone's coffee in the drive-thru, compliment the cashier on their shirt, or tell the receptionist she has pretty eyes. Make someone feel good about themselves today, and you'll feel better in return. Danielle

Most people have heard the expression "acts of kindness," yet few consider implementing them into their daily lives. Performing an act of kindness often has no cost other than being considerate and compassionate toward others. A small act of empathy or offering a listening ear can be a far-reaching gesture that requires nothing but your attention and care for another person.

Giving compliments is one of my favorite ways to brighten someone's day. I might admire someone's jewelry or mention how great a particular color looks on them. If we go out of our way to say something that makes them smile, and base it on what we notice, it can really lift someone's mood and self-esteem. People just want to feel seen; when we notice them and make positive comments, it can make them feel more validated and valued. Small gestures can make a huge difference. When we offer and ask, "How can I help you?" it shows that we care. Being patient and compassionate are also important aspects of thoughtfulness. If you see someone struggling or having a tough day, simply saying, "I'm here if you need to vent," can make all the difference in their day. We often think that being good to others costs something, but generosity doesn't have a price tag. It is in the little gestures, positive words, and small ways of showing that we care.

We can begin by being aware of it. When we look at our own behaviors and take issue with ourselves when we are not being considerate, that is a step. We must be willing to take a different approach to the negativity in our lives that surrounds us. Sometimes, we have more frustrating and tougher days than good ones, but we should avoid taking out our feelings on other people. Becoming mindful before we react can be a way to express warmth because it prevents a lousy exchange before it ever happens.

As I've gotten older, I've become more mindful about the impact of selfish decisions. I had to recognize that in order to be kind to others, I had to start showing kindness to myself. If we are in a good place before we try to help others and take care of our own well-being, we are only filling the cup so we can pour out compassion to others and give from ourselves. We can't pour from an empty cup.

Starting each day with a positive mindset—though not always easy—can help us actively seek out the good in others. Compliments are simple yet powerful. Even saying something like, "I really hope you're having a good day," can open the door to restoring someone's faith in humanity. Wouldn't it be amazing to be the reason someone begins to believe in kindness again?

We don't always know what hardships may affect that cashier's life, the restaurant's server, or the aide who walks us back to set us up for our doctor's appointment. Showing a smile and looking for a way to make their day better helps you and them.

Another simple yet powerful act of kindness is saying "thank you." Two words that are often taken for granted, yet a great way to brighten someone's day. Expressing gratitude when someone holds the door open for you, or maybe was energetic and mowed your front lawn after their own was done, recognizes their effort and shows appreciation. A lot of people say it too often and don't mean it, while some others forget to say it at all. But when we take a moment to genuinely say thanks, it lets someone know their actions mattered. That type of recognition reminds them they're seen and valued.

Gratitude is one of the simplest, most beautiful ways to spread positivity. It costs nothing and takes only a moment. Yet, it has the power to create a ripple effect. What some call "paying it forward" can begin in something as simple as consistently showing appreciation and respect. We each individually help build a more caring, connected, and loving world. And in doing so, we just might inspire others to do the same.

If you buy somebody's coffee at Starbucks or see a lady sitting alone at the restaurant and say, "Please give me her check as well, and don't tell her who paid for it," it can be a powerful example of passing along goodness from the heart. The feeling that you get inside stays with you for a while, and knowing you've impacted another person only reinforces the idea that we all can make this world a better place and can do so just by what you contribute.

There is a lot more negativity surrounding our lives than positivity. This makes our circumstances very difficult and toxic. It can be very hard to even want to be kind. When we deal with an unkind person, be it a rude cashier or an impatient driver on the road, we tend to respond with retaliation instead of empathy. It's not that we necessarily want to react in anger, but we don't always pause and think about how to show our response.

In the same way that we can spread acts of kindness, we can also distribute meanness. How do we react when someone acts rude to us? It's natural to become defensive. If we say something like, "I can see you're having a rough day; I hope it gets better," in a calm, sincere voice, we open the door to more understanding instead of fueling conflict.

Many people are resistant to compassion because they have been taken advantage of in the past. We have to respect our own needs and set boundaries when offering support to others.

We must stay open and honest about it with ourselves and other people. It can be a matter of asking the right questions without being judgmental and expressing a genuine concern, like, "Is there anything I can do to support you?" or "How are you really doing?"

In the long run, every act of kindness we choose will add up. Sometimes, free hugs are all somebody might need. That too can boost our mental health, cause us to feel a little less stressed, and build a connection to other people.

It isn't going to feel natural or normal to consider this whole concept and might even be a whole new thing for you. A great place to start practicing this is within our homes and how we treat the people we live with. When someone offers help without our asking it may surprise us. Sometimes, the people we live with may not expect us to help, and just stepping in to do a little task can relieve stress and improve things at home. It may have been a huge weight lifted that the person did not want to handle because they were tired after a long day. Whether handling a chore like doing the laundry, running an errand, lending a hand, or picking something up on the way home, these small acts of kindness can create harmony in the home. This can extend out to our worldly interactions!

Where can you start implementing more kindness? How does it make you feel to know that you can make a difference simply by showing a more tender attitude – that it could lead us to a better world? If we strive to make every day better for others, we, in return, will reap the benefits. Strive to build up instead of tearing down.

You may have your doubts and wonder if everyone will be on board with this, right? That is okay. Not everybody may want it or think it will work, but it can start with you and me at least giving it a try. It is possible, and it begins with us. This can offer all of us a deeper sense of hope, making kindness something everyone can experience. Let's go and do this!

36

Randomness

Because everything and everyone deserves its place, these misfits certainly earn a chapter of their own! Here is a mix up chapter like those old mix tapes with a little of this and a little of that! Some fun facts, thoughts, or things that just didn't fit well into the other chapters, but I wasn't going to outcast them!

Growing up, I was the tidiest person in the house. My mom didn't impose many chores or expectations on me; I took it upon myself to manage things. Her main request was that I kept my room clean. Mom had a tendency to collect things, and Ed was quite untidy. As a result, cleaning and organizing became my responsibility. In a way, it helped provide some order amid the chaos of my surroundings and our family dynamic.

Slow results are still results—they're progress, just at a different pace.

There You Have It: But Can You Ever Really Tell the Whole Story?

With this book I want people to get a gist of my story, but is it ever possible to capture it all? We miss things, we forget things. We want to make things better or leave some of it out. We pick and choose, but we don't want to lose what we felt was important enough to keep and share.

Tilly's and Tangles: The Back-to-School Shuffle
You might wonder what back-to-school shopping with my kids detailed... nothing too special. I'd always try to take them separately. Andrew was the easy one. The girls, though? They were always very particular in their requests. Honestly, I hated it. I was never smart enough to start early, so it was always a mad dash to get everything done right before school started. We'd zip in and out of stores, even though the whole thing felt like an all-day affair. One nice memory was that we'd always stop for lunch while we were out. The kids had their favorite stores, like Tilly's, and insisted on their specific brands. I hope it's something they remember as somewhat fun for them!

When asked the question, "Am I late, early, or on time?"
    Either or neither. I'm more prompt than I ever used to be when I was younger! But I hate waiting on people for anything! LOL

Must-haves: Chips and lettuce. I also love lunch meat on bread! I buy what's on sale!

Avid reader? I go through periods where I try to read every night... or somewhere. A page or two every day. If I'm reading a book I really love, I'll make extra time for it and finish it faster. Usually, I read in bed or sometimes in my egg chair.

Fun fact - Mom used to read to me—Mary Higgins Clark. Hannah was still a baby when I started reading more.

My favorite genre to read is romance. Romance all the way.

I've never seen a hot air balloon in person!

My most embarrassing moment?
When I was in 6th grade, I was showing off and ran into a pole!

Leisure wear?
My dress-up is a rock band T-shirt and jeans or leggings!

When it's really hot: Air conditioning. Although I love having my windows open and fresh air blowing through.

Talk or Text?
Text. I think it's because I talk so much. Hehe.

It's been a wild ride, but it's helped me so much in my journey. I continue to evolve every day and learn not to take things personally. There are many more pros in life than cons. It's all in the way we perceive it, and sometimes we have to choose to call it as it is.

In terms of legacy, what do I want to be remembered for?

I want people to really think back and say, "She made it. She was a loving mother and sacrificed, all the while trying to become a better version of herself."

I want to be remembered for the hard work I put into bettering myself. I believe we are all here for a reason. Our path is predetermined. It's our journey, and we grow from it. We're still learning until it's time to go. Everything has its purpose for us. We've benefited from what we've been through, and some of us are still here to tell our stories.

Mostly, I want my kids to be proud of me. I want them to know who I am.

I would love to do more things and have the knack for seeing and envisioning them. I'd love to give ideas for new things, and I would do more with redecorating if I had the time, and help others too. I love coming up with things, themes, and changing rooms around.

Do I have a bucket list?
 Not really. I believe it just sets you up for failure.

At the end of the day, we're all just a hot mess in progress. But hey—we've still got blood pumping through our veins, and that alone is something to be grateful for. If you figure it all out before I do, let me know—like, who said what, did we bring snacks, is there enough gas in the car, and did we accidentally take a detour or are we right on track? Either way, maybe it was fabulous. Or maybe it wasn't.
Sometimes we show up and overshare, sometimes we don't share enough. But if we didn't know the plan from the start, and we're still here—that means we did okay. So, here's to the real, raw, ridiculous—crazy, beautiful, messy—life. One minute it's the kids or Dan, the next it's Ed, then it's the bill I forgot to pay because, of course, no reminder came. That's the rhythm. That's real life.
And you know what? Life's actually pretty okay after all.
Remember: You've got this. And you've got me—somewhere out there, lurking on social media, always ready to pump up the fun if you need it.

And before you come to the end of the book, I'm not done yet.

Many of you may have been wondering why your name wasn't mentioned specifically. Like that's it? Please know this: it's not because you weren't remembered. The truth is, it's impossible to name every single person who has made a difference in my life—because there are so many of you. Whether you were part of my past, stand with me in the present, or will walk with me into the future. This is the moment I smiled and thought of you. The story didn't begin here, and in this book, I've only just begun to scratch the surface—the basics, the building blocks, the memories that laid the foundation. But the story doesn't end here either because it's an ongoing journey. There are still so much more memories to celebrate, people to honor, and stories I look forward to sharing. Even if your name isn't printed on these pages, please know this: it's stitched into the tapestry of my life and my heart.

So go ahead... see yourself here.

I dedicate this space to you, right here on this page—because you matter.

There you have it.

About the authors

Danielle Behar Salinger lives in Elk Grove, California, though her heart still holds deep roots in Tennessee, where she was born. After spending a decade working in daycare, Danielle transitioned to life as a stay-at-home mom and, alongside her husband Dan, now serves as the primary caregiver for her beloved father-in-law, Ed. She's also a thriving social media influencer with a loyal and growing following—and now proudly adds "book author" to her list of accomplishments.

Danielle shares her home with her husband Dan, their children, her father-in-law Ed, and their fur family, including dogs, cats, and the unforgettable Millie the pig. As her online presence grew, she realized how easily stories could be misunderstood or misrepresented. That realization inspired her to open up and share her personal journey more authentically. In this book, written in collaboration with Kristi, Danielle tells her truth with honesty, vulnerability, and heart.

When she's not juggling family life, caring for Ed, managing the household, or tending to the pets, you'll likely find Danielle lost in a good book, binge-watching her favorite shows, or enjoying a bit of retail therapy at TJ Maxx, HomeGoods, or Costco. She also has a passion for thrift shopping and lives for the thrill of a great find. One of her favorite roles is being an auntie, she treasures the time spent with her nephews and nieces and the special bond they share. Whether engaging with her Zoomies or connecting with her online followers, Danielle brings warmth, humor, and authenticity to everything she does.

Connect with Danielle:

Explore all the ways to connect with Danielle on her Linktree at: https://linktr.ee/dsalinger50

Follow on YouTube: Danielle Salinger   @Mrsdsalnorcal

Danielle's merchandise store: SABmerch.com
(Shirts, hats, mugs, and more)

Facebook: Danielle Salinger (Look for the certified blue stamp with checkmark)
Instagram: salingerdanielle (look for the verified blue stamp with checkmark)
Tiktok: Danielle Behar Salin   @mrsdsalnorcal

About the authors (Part 2)

Kristi Lyons is a passionate blogger, author, and emerging screenwriter with a compelling voice in nonfiction, inspirational writing, and romantic fiction. She holds a bachelor's degree in creative writing and brings 25 years of experience in healthcare, specifically managing switchboard operations. Kristi blends creative vision with real-world insight, crafting stories that resonate with authenticity and heart.

From early poems and play scripts that were brought to life on stage to leading her high school newspaper as copy and co-editor-in-chief, Kristi has always used words to inspire. Today, she channels that lifelong passion into stories that uplift and empower while speaking to the heart of life's real challenges and triumphs.

In addition to her writing, Kristi is an experienced content creator, writing coach, and workshop facilitator, known for her warm, grounded approach to personal and professional growth. Her current projects include several book releases and screenplay collaborations with industry professionals. She also runs multiple writing-focused pages on social media, where she shares inspiration, encouragement, and a deep love for storytelling.

Away from the keyboard, Kristi lives in upstate New York with her husband, children, and their four beloved corgis, who are never far from her side. She's deeply rooted in her faith and actively involved in her church and community. She finds joy in yard sales, singing, travel, camping, and spending quality time with loved ones.

Connect with Kristi:

Visit her website at: ItsallwritewithKristi.com

Follow on Facebook: Kristi Lyons, Writer

Explore more links and content at https://linktr.ee/kristilyonswriting

Instagram: Kristi Klenchik Lyons

Tiktok: @theturtleneckwrit   OR   @kristiklenchiklyons

Substack: https://substack.com/@kristilyons

Acknowledgements

I want to express my deepest gratitude to Kristi Lyons for seeing the unseen things inside of me. She believed in me and my words from the very beginning. Kristi was the one who said, "Let's do this and make an impact on the world." She saw so much value in my story and encouraged me to dig deep and bring out those under the surface places that became the heart of this book. Her unwavering support, both for me and the community I hope to build, has been invaluable. I'm especially grateful for the countless hours we spent planning, outlining, and brainstorming together.

I'm also incredibly thankful for her help in refining the content, writing, and editing, as well as the resources and support from the incredible people behind the scenes who worked alongside her to help bring this book to life.

To those amazing women I've met on this journey. Your friendship is an everyday source of strength and inspiration. It reminds me that we don't have to walk this path alone. Each one of you has made this journey more meaningful to me. The kindness, honesty, and your unwavering belief in me has been a foundation I've built upon. Thank you for being the true essence of what makes this all worth it.

And to the guys who follow and support me - seriously, thanks for being there even when you could be doing, well, that guy stuff! It's pretty cool that you see something in me that resonates with you and is in tune with my beat!

You all accept me for who I am and make it all worth the while. Every moment, every challenge, and every victory is brighter because of your love and support.

Closing Thoughts

What's next?

Danielle and Kristi are excited about future collaborations, including the possibility of more books and workbooks to accompany their work. Keep an eye out for what's to come!

Through their writing, Danielle and Kristi aim to inspire courage, kindness, and a sense of belonging in their readers. They're both committed to making a positive impact through storytelling and look forward to sharing more with the world in the near future.

Thank You!

A Personal Note From Danielle

Thank you for taking the time to read There You Have It: A Real Raw Candid Look Into My Crazy Life. I truly appreciate your support and for allowing me to share some of my journey with you. It means the world to me that you've taken the time to dive into the pages of this book and that you've walked alongside me through the highs, lows, and everything in between. None of us are alone in the reality that life is messy, but it still can be beautiful, with a ton of unpredictability. Just remember that it's ours to live fully. I hope that my story has inspired you to embrace your own path, celebrate your victories, and learn from your struggles. We are all stronger than we realize, and sometimes, sharing our truth with others is the most powerful thing we can do.

Thank you for being part of this journey with me. Now, it's your turn to keep showing up, living boldly, and doing it your way.

With love and gratitude,
Danielle Behar Salinger

THERE YOU HAVE IT

There you have it!

Have a great day!

Have a smile!

Have a moment to yourself.

Have it, hold it, share it.

This is joy.

That is love.

Made in United States
Cleveland, OH
08 May 2025